FHG

Family Breaks

in Britain

)09

- Fa COUTTS   SLO   £7.99
- Inc

Br es

Botany

2

Maps: ©MAPS IN MINUTES™ / Collins Bartholomew 2007

Typeset by FHG Guides Ltd, Paisley.
Printed and bound in China by Imago.

Distribution. Book Trade: ORCA Book Services, Stanley House,
3 Fleets Lane, Poole, Dorset BH15 3AJ
Tel: 01202 665432; Fax: 01202 666219
e-mail: mail@orcabookservices.co.uk

Published by FHG Guides Ltd., Abbey Mill Business Centre,
Seedhill, Paisley PA1 ITJ
Tel: 0141-887 0428; Fax: 0141-889 7204
e-mail: admin@fhguides.co.uk

Family Breaks in Britain is published by FHG Guides Ltd,
part of Kuperard Group.

Cover design: FHG Guides
Cover Pictures: Woodlands Leisure Park, Dartmouth, Devon
                     www.woodlandspark.com

Acknowledgements

Our thanks for pictures courtesy of:

Thanet Tourism, Britain on View, Rod Edwards (p1, 41),
Woodlands Leisure Park (p65)
Poole Tourism (p92),
Eastbourne Borough Council (p106),
PDPhoto.org (p117)
Scarborough Borough Council (p138),
Blackpool Borough Council Tourism (p145)

Contents

How To Use This Guide

The guide offers information on good beaches, resorts and visits, plus comprehensive coverage of Family Holiday Accommodation.

The order is geographical, starting with Cornwall and working eastwards through Devon, Somerset, Dorset and around the South Coast to London before moving northwards to Scotland, and then to Wales.

For 2009 we have once again included our Vouchers with FREE and REDUCED RATE entry to holiday attractions throughout the country. See pages 9-40.

Detailed page references are provided on contents page 3.

Summarised accommodation listings with detailed information in symbol form appear at the end of each region. This easy reference guide will help you to make preliminary selections, if you wish, of the kind of accommodation and facilities which you feel are most suitable.

On pages 178-181 we once again include the supplement, "Family Friendly Pubs, Inns and Hotels", a brief list of some establishments which have indicated that they particularly welcome children. Please note that not all the hotels/inns featured here have advertisements in this Guide.

A useful index of towns and the sections in which they appear is featured on page 182

KEY TO SYMBOLS

BOARD

total no. bedrooms
with private/en suite facilities
Bed, Breakfast & Evening Meal
BB Bed & Breakfast
Children's meals available
Baby listening

SELF-CATERING

Flats/Apartments
Caravans
Chalets/Lodges
Cottages/Houses
Linen provided
Linen for hire
On site shop

GENERAL

Cots
Highchairs
Laundry facilities available
Indoor play area
Outdoor play area
Pets allowed
Disabled access

Licensed bar
Indoor heated pool
Outdoor heated pool
W Wi-fi access
A Open all year
Totally non-smoking

Ratings & Awards

For the first time ever the AA, VisitBritain, VisitScotland, and the Wales Tourist Board will use a single method of assessing and rating serviced accommodation. Irrespective of which organisation inspects an establishment the rating awarded will be the same, using a common set of standards, giving a clear guide of what to expect. The RAC is no longer operating an Hotel inspection and accreditation business.

Accommodation Standards: Star Grading Scheme

Using a scale of 1-5 stars the objective quality ratings give a clear indication of accommodation standard, cleanliness, ambience, hospitality, service and food, This shows the full range of standards suitable for every budget and preference, and allows visitors to distinguish between the quality of accommodation and facilities on offer in different establishments. All types of board and self-catering accommodation are covered, including hotels, B&Bs, holiday parks, campus accommodation, hostels, caravans and camping, and boats.

VisitBritain and the regional tourist boards, enjoyEngland.com, VisitScotland and VisitWales, and the AA have full details of the grading system on their websites

The more stars, the higher level of quality

★★★★★
exceptional quality, with a degree of luxury

★★★★
excellent standard throughout

★★★
very good level of quality and comfort

★★
good quality, well presented and well run

★
acceptable quality; simple, practical, no frills

National Accessible Scheme

If you have particular mobility, visual or hearing needs, look out for the National Accessible Scheme. You can be confident of finding accommodation or attractions that meet your needs by looking for the following symbols.

 Typically suitable for a person with sufficient mobility to climb a flight of steps but would benefit from fixtures and fittings to aid balance

 Typically suitable for a person with restricted walking ability and for those that may need to use a wheelchair some of the time and can negotiate a maximum of three steps

 Typically suitable for a person who depends on the use of a wheelchair and transfers unaided to and from the wheelchair in a seated position. This person may be an independent traveller

 Typically suitable for a person who depends on the use of a wheelchair in a seated position. This person also requires personal or mechanical assistance (eg carer, hoist).

England and Wales · Counties

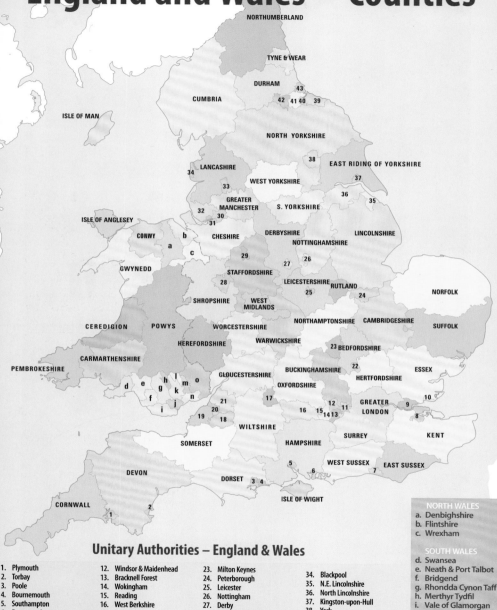

NORTHUMBERLAND
TYNE & WEAR
DURHAM
CUMBRIA
43
42 41 40 39
ISLE OF MAN
NORTH YORKSHIRE
38
LANCASHIRE
34
EAST RIDING OF YORKSHIRE
37
WEST YORKSHIRE
33
36
35
GREATER MANCHESTER
32
30
31
S. YORKSHIRE
ISLE OF ANGLESEY
CONWY
b
a
c
CHESHIRE
DERBYSHIRE
NOTTINGHAMSHIRE
LINCOLNSHIRE
29
27 26
GWYNEDD
STAFFORDSHIRE
28
LEICESTERSHIRE
25
RUTLAND
24
NORFOLK
CEREDIGION
POWYS
SHROPSHIRE
WEST MIDLANDS
WORCESTERSHIRE
NORTHAMPTONSHIRE
CAMBRIDGESHIRE
SUFFOLK
HEREFORDSHIRE
WARWICKSHIRE
23 BEDFORDSHIRE
CARMARTHENSHIRE
22
HERTFORDSHIRE
ESSEX
PEMBROKESHIRE
GLOUCESTERSHIRE
BUCKINGHAMSHIRE
d e g h l m o
f
g
k
i
j
n
OXFORDSHIRE
12 11
16 15 14 13
GREATER LONDON
9
10
8
21
20
18
17
WILTSHIRE
SURREY
KENT
19
SOMERSET
HAMPSHIRE
DEVON
DORSET
3 4
5
6
WEST SUSSEX
7
EAST SUSSEX
CORNWALL
1
2
ISLE OF WIGHT

Unitary Authorities – England & Wales

1. Plymouth
2. Torbay
3. Poole
4. Bournemouth
5. Southampton
6. Portsmouth
7. Brighton & Hove
8. Medway
9. Thurrock
10. Southend
11. Slough
12. Windsor & Maidenhead
13. Bracknell Forest
14. Wokingham
15. Reading
16. West Berkshire
17. Swindon
18. Bath & Northeast Somerset
19. North Somerset
20. Bristol
21. South Gloucestershire
22. Luton
23. Milton Keynes
24. Peterborough
25. Leicester
26. Nottingham
27. Derby
28. Telford & Wrekin
29. Stoke-on-Trent
30. Warrington
31. Halton
32. Merseyside
33. Blackburn with Darwen
34. Blackpool
35. N.E. Lincolnshire
36. North Lincolnshire
37. Kingston-upon-Hull
38. York
39. Redcar & Cleveland
40. Middlesborough
41. Stockton-on-Tees
42. Darlington
43. Hartlepool

NORTH WALES
a. Denbighshire
b. Flintshire
c. Wrexham

SOUTH WALES
d. Swansea
e. Neath & Port Talbot
f. Bridgend
g. Rhondda Cynon Taff
h. Merthyr Tydfil
i. Vale of Glamorgan
j. Cardiff
k. Caerphilly
l. Blaenau Gwent
m. Torfaen
n. Newport
o. Monmouthshire

FHG ·K·U·P·E·R·A·R·D· READERS' OFFER 2009

MUSEUM OF LONDON DOCKLANDS
No1 Warehouse, West India Quay, London E14 4AL
Tel: 0870 444 3855 • e-mail: info@museumoflondon.org.uk
www.museumoflondon.org.uk

This voucher entitles the bearer to TWO full price adult tickets for the price of ONE on presentation at the Museum of London Docklands admission desk. A max. of one person goes free per voucher. Offer valid until 31 Dec. 2009. Only one voucher per transaction. Non-transferable and non-exchangeable. No cash alternative. Subject to availability. Tickets allow unlimited entry for one year. Children enter free as standard all year round.

NOT TO BE USED IN CONJUNCTION WITH ANY OTHER OFFER

FHG ·K·U·P·E·R·A·R·D· READERS' OFFER 2009

LEIGHTON BUZZARD RAILWAY
Page's Park Station, Billington Road,
Leighton Buzzard, Bedfordshire LU7 4TN
Tel: 01525 373888
e-mail: station@lbngrs.org.uk
www.buzzrail.co.uk

One FREE adult/child with full-fare adult ticket
Valid 15/3/2009 - 8/11/2009

NOT TO BE USED IN CONJUNCTION WITH ANY OTHER OFFER

FHG ·K·U·P·E·R·A·R·D· READERS' OFFER 2009

BUCKINGHAMSHIRE RAILWAY CENTRE
Quainton Road Station, Quainton,
Aylesbury HP22 4BY
Tel & Fax: 01296 655720
e-mail: bucksrailcentre@btconnect.com
www.bucksrailcentre.org

One child FREE with each full-paying adult
Not valid for Special Events

NOT TO BE USED IN CONJUNCTION WITH ANY OTHER OFFER

FHG ·K·U·P·E·R·A·R·D· READERS' OFFER 2009

BEKONSCOT MODEL VILLAGE & RAILWAY
Warwick Road, Beaconsfield,
Buckinghamshire HP9 2PL
Tel: 01494 672919
e-mail: info@bekonscot.co.uk
www.bekonscot.com

One child FREE when accompanied by full-paying adult
Valid February to October 2009

NOT TO BE USED IN CONJUNCTION WITH ANY OTHER OFFER

From Roman settlement to Dockland's regeneration, unlock the history of London's river, port and people in this historic West India Quay warehouse. Discover a wealth of objects, from whalebones to WWII gas masks, in state-of-the-art galleries, including Mudlarks, an interactive area for children; Sailortown, an atmospheric re-creation of 19thC riverside Wapping; and London, Sugar & Slavery, which reveals the city's involvement in the transatlantic slave trade.

Open: daily 10am-6pm. Closed 24-26 December.

Directions: 2 minutes' walk from West India Quay. Nearest Tube Canary Wharf.

A 70-minute journey into the lost world of the English narrow gauge light railway. Features historic steam locomotives from many countries.

PETS MUST BE KEPT UNDER CONTROL AND NOT ALLOWED ON TRACKS

Open: Sundays and Bank Holiday weekends 22 March to 25 October. Additional days in summer.

Directions: on south side of Leighton Buzzard. Follow brown signs from town centre or A505/A4146 bypass.

A working steam railway centre. Steam train rides, miniature railway rides, large collection of historic preserved steam locomotives, carriages and wagons.

Open: daily April to October 10.30am to 4.30pm. Variable programme - check website or call.

Directions: off A41 Aylesbury to Bicester Road, 6 miles north west of Aylesbury.

Be a giant in a magical miniature world of make-believe depicting rural England in the 1930s. "A little piece of history that is forever England."

Open: 10am-5pm daily mid February to end October.

Directions: Junction 16 M25, Junction 2 M40.

FHG
·K·U·P·E·R·A·R·D·
READERS' OFFER 2009

THE RAPTOR FOUNDATION
The Heath, St Ives Road,
Woodhurst, Huntingdon, Cambs PE28 3BT
Tel: 01487 741140 • Fax: 01487 841140
e-mail: heleowl@aol.com
www.raptorfoundation.org.uk

TWO for the price of ONE
Valid until end 2009 (not Bank Holidays)

NOT TO BE USED IN CONJUNCTION WITH ANY OTHER OFFER

FHG
·K·U·P·E·R·A·R·D·
READERS' OFFER 2009

FLAG FEN ARCHAEOLOGY PARK
The Droveway, Northey Road,
Peterborough, Cambs PE6 7QJ
Tel: 0844 414 0646 • Fax: 0844 414 0647
e-mail: info@flagfen.org
www.flagfen.org

20% off normal entry price. Valid 1st March-31st Oct 2009
Not for special events or ticketed events.

NOT TO BE USED IN CONJUNCTION WITH ANY OTHER OFFER

FHG
·K·U·P·E·R·A·R·D·
READERS' OFFER 2009

ANSON ENGINE MUSEUM
Anson Road, Poynton,
Cheshire SK12 1TD
Tel: 01625 874426
e-mail: enquiry@enginemuseum.org
www.enginemuseum.org

Saturdays - 2 for 1 entry (when one of equal or greater
value is purchased). Valid 12 April-30 Sept 2009

NOT TO BE USED IN CONJUNCTION WITH ANY OTHER OFFER

FHG
·K·U·P·E·R·A·R·D·
READERS' OFFER 2009

BRITISH CYCLING MUSEUM
The Old Station,
Camelford,
Cornwall PL32 9TZ
Tel: 01840 212811
www.camelford.org

Child FREE with one paying adult
Valid during 2009

NOT TO BE USED IN CONJUNCTION WITH ANY OTHER OFFER

Birds of Prey Centre offering audience participation in flying displays which are held 3 times daily. Tours, picnic area, gift shop, tearoom, craft shop.

Open: 10am-5pm all year except Christmas and New Year.

Directions: follow brown tourist signs from B1040.

Home to a unique ancient wooden monument, a km long causeway and platform, perfectly preserved in the wetland. Originally built from 60,000 upright timbers and 250,000 horizontal timbers. Also visit roundhouses, fields and museum.

Open: March to October 10am to 5pm Tuesday to Sunday. Last entry 4pm.

Directions: by bicycle or on foot from the Green Wheel. By car from J5 of A1139, Peterborough ring road, then follow the brown signs.

As seen on TV, this multi award-winning attraction has a great deal to offer visitors. It houses the largest collection of engines in Europe, local history area, craft centre (bodging and smithy work), with changing exhibitions throughout the season.

Open: Easter Sunday until end October, Friday to Sunday and Bank Holidays, 10am to 5pm.

Directions: approx 7 miles from J1 M60 and 9 miles J3 M60. Follow brown tourist signs from Poynton traffic lights.

The nation's foremost and largest museum of historic cycling, with over 400 examples of cycles, and 1000s of items of cycling memorabilia.

Open: all year, Sunday to Thursday, 10am to 5pm.

Directions: one mile north of Camelford, B3266/B3314 crossroads.

FHG K·U·P·E·R·A·R·D
READERS'
OFFER
2009

CHINA CLAY COUNTRY PARK
Wheal Martyn, Carthew, St Austell,
Cornwall PL26 8XG
Tel & Fax: 01726 850362
e-mail: info@chinaclaycountry.co.uk
www.chinaclaycountry.co.uk

TWO for ONE adult entry, saving £7.50.
One voucher per person. Valid until July 2009.

NOT TO BE USED IN CONJUNCTION WITH ANY OTHER OFFER

FHG K·U·P·E·R·A·R·D

READERS'
OFFER
2009

NATIONAL LOBSTER HATCHERY
South Quay, Padstow,
Cornwall PL28 8BL
Tel: 01841 533877 • Fax: 0870 7060299
e-mail: info@nationallobsterhatchery.co.uk
www.nationallobsterhatchery.co.uk

TWO for the price of ONE
Valid November 2008 to March 2009

NOT TO BE USED IN CONJUNCTION WITH ANY OTHER OFFER

FHG K·U·P·E·R·A·R·D

READERS'
OFFER
2009

NATIONAL SEAL SANCTUARY
Gweek, Helston,
Cornwall TR12 6UG
Tel: 01326 221361
e-mail: seals@sealsanctuary.co.uk
www.sealsanctuary.co.uk

TWO for ONE - on purchase of another ticket of
equal or greater value. Valid until December 2009.

NOT TO BE USED IN CONJUNCTION WITH ANY OTHER OFFER

FHG K·U·P·E·R·A·R·D

READERS'
OFFER
2009

PORFELL WILDLIFE PARK & SANCTUARY
Trecangate, Near Llanreath,
Liskeard,
Cornwall PL14 4RE
Tel: 01503 220211
www.porfellanimalland.co.uk

One child FREE with one paying adult per voucher
Valid 1st April-31st October 2009.

NOT TO BE USED IN CONJUNCTION WITH ANY OTHER OFFER

The Country Park covers 26 acres and includes woodland and historic trails, picnic sites, children's adventure trail and award-winning cycle trail. Remains of a Victorian clay works complete with the largest working water wheel in Cornwall. Shop, cafe, exhibitions, museum.

Open: 10am-6pm daily (closed Christmas Day)

Directions: two miles north of St Austell on the B3274. Follow brown tourist signs. 5 minutes from Eden Project.

FHG GUIDES, ABBEY MILL BUSINESS CENTRE, PAISLEY PA1 1TJ • www.holidayguides.com

---

A unique conservation programme - see our fisheries at work and find out everything there is to know about the European lobster.

Open: from 10am seven days a week.

Directions: right on the water's edge, in the South Quay car park, right opposite Rick Stein's fish & chip shop.

FHG GUIDES, ABBEY MILL BUSINESS CENTRE, PAISLEY PA1 1TJ • www.holidayguides.com

---

Britain's leading grey seal rescue centre

Open: daily (except Christmas Day) from 10am

Directions: from A30 follow signs to Helston, then brown tourist signs to Seal Sanctuary.

FHG GUIDES, ABBEY MILL BUSINESS CENTRE, PAISLEY PA1 1TJ • www.holidayguides.com

---

Porfell is home to wild and exotic animals from around the world. Idyllically situated amongst the rolling hills of south east Cornwall. It has a beautiful woodland with raised boardwalks over marsh areas, and a children's farm.

Open: 10am-6pm daily from April 1st to October 31st.

Directions: A38 Liskeard, A390 for St Austell. Turn off at East Taphouse on to B3359, follow brown tourist signs.

FHG GUIDES, ABBEY MILL BUSINESS CENTRE, PAISLEY PA1 1TJ • www.holidayguides.com

Cornwall's only Donkey Sanctuary set in 14 acres overlooking the beautiful Tamar Valley. Donkey rides, goat hill, children's playgrounds, cafe and picnic area. New all-weather play barn.

Open: Easter to end Oct: daily 10am to 5pm. Nov to March: weekends and all school holidays 10.30am to 4.30pm

Directions: just off A390 between Callington and Gunnislake at St Ann's Chapel.

A collection of cars from film and TV, including Chitty Chitty Bang Bang, James Bond's Aston Martin, Del Boy's van, Fab1 and many more.

PETS MUST BE KEPT ON LEAD

Open: daily 10am-5pm. Open February half term, 1st April to end November, also weekends in December.

Directions: in centre of Keswick close to car park.

The Beacon is the Copeland area's interactive museum, tracing the area's rich history, from as far back as prehistoric times to the modern day. Enjoy panoramic views of the Georgian town and harbour from the 4th floor viewing gallery. Art gallery, gift shop, restaurant. Fully accessible.

Open: open all year (excl. 24-26 Dec) Tuesday to Sunday, plus Monday Bank Holidays.

Directions: enter Whitehaven from north or south on A595. Follow the town centre and brown museum signs; located on harbourside.

A superb family day out in the atmosphere of a bygone era. Explore the recreated period street and fascinating exhibitions. Unlimited tram rides are free with entry. Play areas, woodland walk and sculpture trail, shops, tea rooms, pub, restaurant and lots more.

Open: daily April to October 10 am to 5.30pm.

Directions: eight miles from M1 Junction 28, follow brown and white signs for "Tramway Museum".

FHG
·K·U·P·E·R·A·R·D·
READERS' OFFER 2009

POOLE'S CAVERN & BUXTON COUNTRY PARK
Green Lane, Buxton,
Derbyshire Sk17 9DH
Tel: 01298 26978 • Fax: 01298 73563
e-mail: info@poolescavern.co.uk
www.poolescavern.co.uk

*20% off standard entry price to Poole's Cavern.
Not valid for special events. Valid during 2009.*

FHG
·K·U·P·E·R·A·R·D·
READERS' OFFER 2009

WOODLANDS
Blackawton, Dartmouth,
Devon TQ9 7DQ
Tel: 01803 712598 • Fax: 01803 712680
e-mail: fun@woodlandspark.com
www.woodlandspark.com

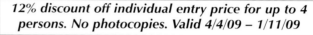

*12% discount off individual entry price for up to 4
persons. No photocopies. Valid 4/4/09 – 1/11/09*

FHG
·K·U·P·E·R·A·R·D·
READERS' OFFER 2009

DEVONSHIRE COLLECTION OF PERIOD COSTUME
Totnes Costume Museum,
Bogan House, 43 High Street,
Totnes,
Devon TQ9 5NP

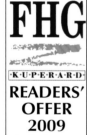

*FREE child with a paying adult with voucher
Valid from Spring Bank Holiday to end of Sept 2009*

FHG
·K·U·P·E·R·A·R·D·
READERS' OFFER 2009

TWEDDLE CHILDREN'S ANIMAL FARM
Fillpoke Lane, Blackhall Colliery,
Co. Durham TS27 4BT
Tel: 0191 586 3311
e-mail: info@tweddle-farm.co.uk
www.tweddle-farm.co.uk

*FREE bag of animal food to every paying customer.
Valid until end 2009*

A spectacular natural cavern set in beautiful woodlands. Explore the crystal-lined chambers with expert guides, deep into the Peak District underground world. Climb to Solomon's Temple viewpoint at the summit of Grin Low.

Open: daily March to November 9.30am to 5pm; winter weekends.

Directions: one mile from Buxton town centre, off A515.

All weather fun - guaranteed! Unique combination of indoor/outdoor attractions. 3 Watercoasters, Toboggan Run, Arctic Gliders, boats, 15 Playzones for all ages. Biggest indoor venture zone in UK with 5 floors of play and rides. Big Fun Farm with U-drive Tractor ride, new Sea Dragon Swing Ship. Falconry Centre.

Open: mid-March to November open daily at 9.30am. Winter: open weekends and local school holidays.

Directions: 5 miles from Dartmouth on A3122. Follow brown tourist signs from A38.

Themed exhibition, changed annually, based in a Tudor house. Collection contains items of dress for women, men and children from 17th century to 1990s, from high fashion to everyday wear.

Open: Open from Spring Bank Holiday to end September. 11am to 5pm Tuesday to Friday.

Directions: centre of town, opposite Market Square. Mini bus up High Street stops outside.

Children's farm and petting centre with lots of farm animals and exotic animals too, including camels, otters, monkeys, meerkats and lots more. Lots of hands-on, with bottle feeding, reptile handling and bunny cuddling happening daily.

Open: March to Oct: 10am-5pm daily; Nov to Feb 10am to 4pm daily. Closed Christmas, Boxing Day and New Year's Day.

Directions: A181 from A19, head towards coast; signposted from there.

BARLEYLANDS FARM & CRAFT VILLAGE
**Barleylands Road, Billericay,
Essex CM11 2UD**
Tel: 01268 290229 • Fax: 01268 290222
e-mail: info@barleylands.co.uk
www.barleylands.co.uk

**READERS'
OFFER
2009**

*FREE entry for one child with each full paying adult
Valid during 2009*

NOT TO BE USED IN CONJUNCTION WITH ANY OTHER OFFER

AVON VALLEY RAILWAY
**Bitton Station, Bath Road, Bitton,
Bristol BS30 6HD**
Tel: 0117 932 5538
e-mail: info@avonvalleyrailway.org
www.avonvalleyrailway.org

**READERS'
OFFER
2009**

*One FREE child with every fare-paying adult
Valid May - Oct 2009 (not 'Day Out with Thomas' events)*

NOT TO BE USED IN CONJUNCTION WITH ANY OTHER OFFER

CIDER MUSEUM & KING OFFA DISTILLERY
**21 Ryelands Street, Hereford,
Herefordshire HR4 0LW**
Tel: 01432 354207
e-mail: enquiries@cidermuseum.co.uk
www.cidermuseum.co.uk

**READERS'
OFFER
2009**

*TWO for the price of ONE admission
Valid to end December 2009*

NOT TO BE USED IN CONJUNCTION WITH ANY OTHER OFFER

MUSEUM OF KENT LIFE
**Lock Lane, Sandling, Maidstone,
Kent ME14 3AU**
Tel: 01622 763936 • Fax: 01622 662024
e-mail: enquiries@museum-kentlife.co.uk
www.museum-kentlife.co.uk

MUSEUM OF KENT LIFE

**READERS'
OFFER
2009**

*One child FREE with one full-paying adult
Valid during 2009*

NOT TO BE USED IN CONJUNCTION WITH ANY OTHER OFFER

Set in over 700 acres of unspoilt Essex countryside, this former working farm is one of the county's most popular tourist attractions. The spectacular craft village and educational farm provide the perfect setting for a great day out.

Open: 7 days a week from 10am-5pm all year except 25/26 December and 1st January

Directions: follow brown tourist signs from A127 and A12.

The Avon Valley Railway offers a whole new experience for some, and a nostalgic memory for others.

PETS MUST BE KEPT ON LEADS AND OFF TRAIN SEATS

Open: Steam trains operate every Sunday, Easter to October, plus Bank Holidays and Christmas.

Directions: on the A431 midway between Bristol and Bath at Bitton.

Learn how traditional cider and perry was made, how the fruit was harvested, milled, pressed and bottled. Walk through original champagne cider cellars, and view 18th century lead crystal cider glasses.

Open: April to October: 10am-5pm Tues-Sat. November to March 11am-3pm Tues-Sat.

Directions: off A438 Hereford to Brecon road, near Sainsbury's supermarket.

Kent's award-winning open air museum is home to a collection of historic buildings which house interactive exhibitions on life over the last 150 years.

Open: seven days a week, February to start November, 10am to 5pm.

Directions: Junction 6 off M20, follow signs to Aylesford.

FHG
K·U·P·E·R·A·R·D
READERS' OFFER 2009

CHISLEHURST CAVES
Old Hill, Chislehurst,
Kent BR7 5NL
Tel: 020 8467 3264 • Fax: 020 8295 0407
e-mail: info@chislehurstcaves.co.uk
www.chislehurstcaves.co.uk

> FREE child entry with full paying adult.
> Valid until end 2009 (not Bank Holiday weekends)

NOT TO BE USED IN CONJUNCTION WITH ANY OTHER OFFER

FHG
K·U·P·E·R·A·R·D
READERS' OFFER 2009

SKEGNESS NATURELAND SEAL SANCTUARY
North Parade, Skegness,
Lincolnshire PE25 1DB
Tel: 01754 764345
e-mail: info@skegnessnatureland.co.uk
www.skegnessnatureland.co.uk

> Free entry for one child when accompanied by
> full-paying adult. Valid during 2009.

NOT TO BE USED IN CONJUNCTION WITH ANY OTHER OFFER

FHG
K·U·P·E·R·A·R·D
READERS' OFFER 2009

BRESSINGHAM STEAM & GARDENS
Low Road, Bressingham, Diss,
Norfolk IP22 2AB
Tel: 01379 686900 • Fax: 01379 686907
e-mail: info@bressingham.co.uk
www.bressingham.co.uk

> One child FREE with two paying adults
> Valid Easter to October 2009 (ref 8175)

NOT TO BE USED IN CONJUNCTION WITH ANY OTHER OFFER

FHG
K·U·P·E·R·A·R·D
READERS' OFFER 2009

NEWARK AIR MUSEUM
The Airfield, Winthorpe, Newark,
Nottinghamshire NG24 2NY
Tel: 01636 707170
e-mail: newarkair@onetel.com
www.newarkairmuseum.org

> Party rate discount for every voucher (50p per person
> off normal admission). Valid during 2009.

NOT TO BE USED IN CONJUNCTION WITH ANY OTHER OFFER

Miles of mystery and history beneath your feet! Grab a lantern and get ready for an amazing underground adventure. Your whole family can travel back in time as you explore this labyrinth of dark mysterious passageways. See the caves, church, Druid altar and more.

Open: Wed to Sun from 10am; last tour 4pm. Open daily during local school and Bank holidays (except Christmas). Entrance by guided tour only.

Directions: A222 between A20 and A21; at Chislehurst Station turn into Station Approach; turn right at end, then right again into Caveside Close.

FHG GUIDES, ABBEY MILL BUSINESS CENTRE, PAISLEY PA1 1TJ • www.holidayguides.com

---

Well known for rescuing and rehabilitating orphaned and injured seal pups found washed ashore on Lincolnshire beaches. Also: penguins, aquarium, pets' corner, reptiles, Floral Palace (tropical birds and butterflies etc).

Open: daily from 10am. Closed Christmas/Boxing/New Year's Days.

Directions: at the north end of Skegness seafront.

FHG GUIDES, ABBEY MILL BUSINESS CENTRE, PAISLEY PA1 1TJ • www.holidayguides.com

---

Explore one of Europe's leading steam collections, take a ride over 5 miles of narrow gauge steam railway, wander through beautiful gardens, or visit the only official 'Dads' Army' exhibition. Two restaurants and garden centre.

Open: Easter to October 10.30am - 5pm

Directions: 2½ miles west of Diss and 14 miles east of Thetford on the A1066; follow brown tourist signs.

FHG GUIDES, ABBEY MILL BUSINESS CENTRE, PAISLEY PA1 1TJ • www.holidayguides.com

---

A collection of 70 aircraft and cockpit sections from across the history of aviation. Extensive aero engine and artefact displays.

Open: daily from 10am (closed Christmas period and New Year's Day).

Directions: follow brown and white signs from A1, A46, A17 and A1133.

FHG GUIDES, ABBEY MILL BUSINESS CENTRE, PAISLEY PA1 1TJ • www.holidayguides.com

Enter and explore these ancient caves and see how the people of Nottingham have used them for over 750 years.

Open: daily 10.30-5pm (tours every half hour).

Directions: in Nottingham city centre on the upper level of Broadmarsh Shopping Centre.

Let us welcome you to Nottingham's notorious county gaol, and once behind bars, our resident ghosts won't want you to leave!

Open: peak season - daily 10am-5pm; off peak Tues - Sun 10am-4pm. Tours every half hour.

Directions: in the heart of the historic Lace Market district, just 10 minutes' walk from train station.

Family-run farm park set in beautiful countryside next to river. 20-acre site with animal handling, large indoor soft play area, go-karts, trampolines, pedal tractors, swings, slides, zipline and assault course. New Jumicar children's driving activity (small extra charge)

Open: daily 10am to 5.30pm April to end September. Closed Mondays except Bank Holidays and during Nottinghamshire school holidays. Please check for winter opening hours.

Directions: off A612 Nottingham to Southwell road.

Travel back in time with Robin Hood and his merry men on an adventure-packed theme tour, exploring the intriguing and mysterious story of their legendary tales of Medieval England. Enjoy film shows, live performances, adventure rides and even try archery! Are you brave enough to join Robin on his quest for good against evil?

Open: 10am-5pm, last admission 4pm.

Directions: follow the brown and white tourist information signs whilst heading towards the city centre.

FLEET AIR ARM MUSEUM
RNAS Yeovilton, Ilchester,
Somerset BA22 8HT
Tel: 01935 840565
e-mail: enquiries@fleetairarm.com
www.fleetairarm.com

Fleet Air Arm Museum

READERS' OFFER 2009

One child FREE with full paying adult
Valid during 2009 except Bank Holidays

NOT TO BE USED IN CONJUNCTION WITH ANY OTHER OFFER

THE HELICOPTER MUSEUM
The Heliport, Locking Moor Road,
Weston-Super-Mare BS24 8PP
Tel: 01934 635227• Fax: 01934 645230
e-mail: helimuseum@btconnect.com
www.helicoptermuseum.co.uk

READERS' OFFER 2009

One child FREE with two full-paying adults
Valid from April to October 2009

NOT TO BE USED IN CONJUNCTION WITH ANY OTHER OFFER

EXMOOR FALCONRY & ANIMAL FARM
Allerford, Near Porlock, Minehead,
Somerset TA24 8HJ
Tel: 01643 862816
e-mail: exmoor.falcon@virgin.net
www.exmoorfalconry.co.uk

Exmoor Falconry

READERS' OFFER 2009

10% off entry to Falconry Centre
Valid during 2009

NOT TO BE USED IN CONJUNCTION WITH ANY OTHER OFFER

EASTON FARM PARK
Pound Corner, Easton, Woodhouse,
Suffolk IP13 0EQ
Tel: 01728 746475
e-mail: info@eastonfarmpark.co.uk
www.eastonfarmpark.co.uk

Easton Farm Park

READERS' OFFER 2009

One FREE child entry with a full paying adult
Only one voucher per group. Valid during 2009.

NOT TO BE USED IN CONJUNCTION WITH ANY OTHER OFFER

Europe's largest naval aviation collection with over 40 aircraft on display , including Concorde 002 and Ark Royal Aircraft Carrier Experience. Situated on an operational naval air station.

Open: open daily April to October 10am-5.30pm; November to March 10am-4.30pm (closed Mon and Tues).

Directions: just off A303/A37 on B3151 at Ilchester. Yeovil rail station 10 miles.

The world's largest helicopter collection - over 70 exhibits, includes two royal helicopters, Russian Gunship and Vietnam veterans plus many award-winning exhibits. Cafe, shop. Flights.

PETS MUST BE KEPT UNDER CONTROL

Open: Wednesday to Sunday 10am to 5.30pm. Daily during school Easter and Summer holidays and Bank Holiday Mondays. November to March: 10am to 4.30pm

Directions: Junction 21 off M5 then follow the propellor signs.

Falconry centre with animals - flying displays, animal handling, feeding and bottle feeding - in 15th century NT farmyard setting on Exmoor. Also falconry and outdoor activities, hawk walks and riding.

Open: 10.30am to 5pm daily

Directions: A39 west of Minehead, turn right at Allerford, half a mile along lane on left.

Family day out down on the farm, with activities for children every half hour (included in entry price). Indoor and outdoor play areas. Riverside cafe, gift shop. For more details visit the website.

Open: 10.30am-6pm daily March to September.

Directions: signposted from A12 in the direction of Framlingham.

Stories of racing, ride the horse simulator, or take a 'behind the scenes' tour of the training grounds and yards.

Open: Easter to end October, 7 days a week 11am to 5pm. Last admission 4pm.

Directions: on the High Street in the centre of Newmarket.

FHG GUIDES, ABBEY MILL BUSINESS CENTRE, PAISLEY PA1 1TJ • www.holidayguides.com

---

3 attractions in 1.
Tropical butterflies, exotic animals of many types in our Noah's Ark Rescue Centre. Theme gardens with a free competition for kids. Rejectamenta - the nostalgia museum.

Open: 10am - 6pm daily late March to end October.

Directions: signposted from A27/A286 junction at Chichester.

FHG GUIDES, ABBEY MILL BUSINESS CENTRE, PAISLEY PA1 1TJ • www.holidayguides.com

---

Hatton Farm Village offers a wonderful mix of farmyard animals, adventure play, shows, demonstrations, and events, all set in the stunning Warwickshire countryside.

Open: daily 10am-5pm (4pm during winter). Closed Christmas Day and Boxing Day.

Directions: 5 minutes from M40 (J15), A46 towards Coventry, then just off A4177 (follow brown tourist signs).

FHG GUIDES, ABBEY MILL BUSINESS CENTRE, PAISLEY PA1 1TJ • www.holidayguides.com

---

Birds of prey centre with over 60 birds including owls, hawks, falcons, kites, vultures and eagles. 3 flying displays daily.
When possible public welcome to handle birds after each display. No dogs allowed.

Open: 1st March to 31st October 10.30am to 5.30pm. Flying displays 11.30am, 1.30pm and 3.30pm daily.

Directions: on the A167 between Northallerton and the Ripon turn off. Follow brown tourist signs.

FHG GUIDES, ABBEY MILL BUSINESS CENTRE, PAISLEY PA1 1TJ • www.holidayguides.com

29

All types of birds of prey exhibited here, from owls and kestrels to eagles and vultures. Special flying displays 12 noon, 1.30pm and 3pm. Winter shows 12noon and 1.30pm. Bird handling courses arranged for either half or full days.

GUIDE DOGS ONLY

Open: 10am to 4.30pm summer 10am to 4pm winter

Directions: on main A65 trunk road outside Settle. Follow brown direction signs.

Visit James Herriot's original house recreated as it was in the 1940s. Television sets used in the series 'All Creatures Great and Small'. There is a children's interactive gallery with life-size model farm animals and three rooms dedicated to the history of veterinary medicine.

Open: daily. Easter-Oct 10am-5pm; Nov-Easter 11am to 4pm

Directions: follow signs off A1 or A19 to Thirsk, then A168, off Thirsk market place

A fascinating display of railway carriages and a wide range of railway items telling the story of rail travel over the years.

ALL PETS MUST BE KEPT ON LEADS

Open: daily 11am to 4.30pm

Directions: approximately one mile from Keighley on A629 Halifax road. Follow brown tourist signs

As the UK's National Children's Museum, Eureka! is a place where children play to learn and grown-ups learn to play.

Open: daily except 24-26 December, 10am to 5pm

Directions: leave M62 at J24 for Halifax. Take A629 to town centre, following brown tourist signs.

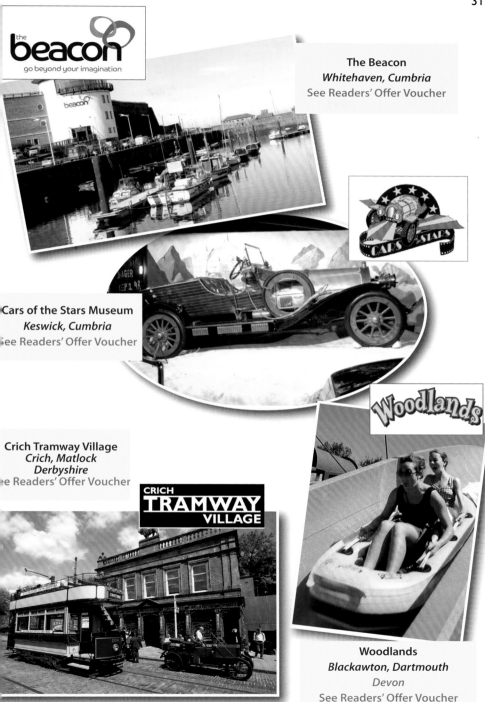

The Beacon
Whitehaven, Cumbria
See Readers' Offer Voucher

Cars of the Stars Museum
Keswick, Cumbria
See Readers' Offer Voucher

Crich Tramway Village
Crich, Matlock
Derbyshire
See Readers' Offer Voucher

Woodlands
Blackawton, Dartmouth
Devon
See Readers' Offer Voucher

Galloway Wildlife Conservation Park
Lochfergus, Kirkcudbright,
Dumfries & Galloway
See Readers' Offer Voucher

Llanberis Lake Railway
Gilfach Ddu, Llanberis, Gwynedd
See Readers' Offer Voucher

33

FHG ·K·U·P·E·R·A·R·D· **READERS' OFFER 2009**

THE GRASSIC GIBBON CENTRE
Arbuthnott, Laurencekirk,
Aberdeenshire AB30 1PB
Tel: 01561 361668
e-mail: lgginfo@grassicgibbon.com
www.grassicgibbon.com

TWO for the price of ONE entry to exhibition (based on full adult rate only). Valid during 2009 (not groups)

NOT TO BE USED IN CONJUNCTION WITH ANY OTHER OFFER

FHG ·K·U·P·E·R·A·R·D· **READERS' OFFER 2009**

SCOTTISH MARITIME MUSEUM
Harbourside, Irvine,
Ayrshire KA12 8QE
Tel: 01294 278283
Fax: 01294 313211
www.scottishmaritimemuseum.org

TWO for the price of ONE
Valid from April to October 2009

NOT TO BE USED IN CONJUNCTION WITH ANY OTHER OFFER

FHG ·K·U·P·E·R·A·R·D· **READERS' OFFER 2009**

DALSCONE FARM FUN
Dalscone Farm, Edinburgh Road,
Dumfries DG1 1SE
Tel: 01387 257546 • Shop: 01387 254445
e-mail: dalscone@btconnect.com
www.dalsconefarm.co.uk

One FREE adult (16 years+)
Valid during 2009

NOT TO BE USED IN CONJUNCTION WITH ANY OTHER OFFER

FHG 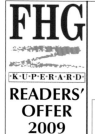 ·K·U·P·E·R·A·R·D· **READERS' OFFER 2009**

GALLOWAY WILDLIFE CONSERVATION PARK
Lochfergus Plantation, Kirkcudbright,
Dumfries & Galloway DG6 4XX
Tel & Fax: 01557 331645
e-mail: info@gallowaywildlife.co.uk
www.gallowaywildlife.co.uk

One FREE child or Senior Citizen with two full paying adults.
Valid Feb - Nov 2009 (not Easter weekend and Bank Holidays)

NOT TO BE USED IN CONJUNCTION WITH ANY OTHER OFFER

Visitor Centre dedicated to the much-loved Scottish writer Lewis Grassic Gibbon. Exhibition, cafe, gift shop. Outdoor children's play area. Disabled access throughout.

Open: daily April to October 10am to 4.30pm. Groups by appointment including evenings.

Directions: on the B967, accessible and signposted from both A90 and A92.

Scotland's seafaring heritage is among the world's richest and you can relive the heyday of Scottish shipping at the Maritime Museum.

Open: 1st April to 31st October - 10am-5pm

Directions: situated on Irvine harbourside and only a 10 minute walk from Irvine train station.

Indoor adventure play area, farm park, toyshop and cafe. A great day out for all the family, with sledge and zip slides, mini-golf, trampolines, bumper boats, pottery painting and so much more.

Open: Monday to Saturday 10am-5.30pm.

Directions: just off the A75/A701 roundabout heading for Moffat and Edinburgh.

The wild animal conservation centre of Southern Scotland. A varied collection of over 150 animals from all over the world can be seen within natural woodland settings. Picnic areas, cafe/gift shop, outdoor play area, woodland walks, close animal encounters.

Open: 10am to dusk 1st February to 30 November.

Directions: follow brown tourist signs from A75; one mile from Kirkcudbright on the B727.

CREETOWN GEM ROCK MUSEUM
**Chain Road, Creetown, Newton Stewart
Dumfries & Galloway DG8 7HJ
Tel: 01671 820357 • Fax: 01671 820554
e-mail: enquiries@gemrock.net
www.gemrock.net**

READERS' OFFER 2009

*10% discount on admission.
Valid during 2009.*

NOT TO BE USED IN CONJUNCTION WITH ANY OTHER OFFER

MYRETON MOTOR MUSEUM
**Aberlady,
East Lothian
EH32 0PZ
Tel: 01875 870288**

MYRETON MOTOR MUSEUM

READERS' OFFER 2009

*One child FREE with each paying adult
Valid during 2009*

NOT TO BE USED IN CONJUNCTION WITH ANY OTHER OFFER

BO'NESS & KINNEIL RAILWAY
**Bo'ness Station, Union Street,
Bo'ness, West Lothian EH51 9AQ
Tel: 01506 822298
e-mail: enquiries.railway@srps.org.uk
www.srps.org.uk**

READERS' OFFER 2009

*FREE child train fare with one paying adult/concession. Valid 29th
March-26th Oct 2009. Not Thomas events or Santa Steam trains*

NOT TO BE USED IN CONJUNCTION WITH ANY OTHER OFFER

BUTTERFLY & INSECT WORLD
**Dobbies Garden World, Melville Nursery,
Lasswade, Midlothian EH18 1AZ
Tel: 0131-663 4932 • Fax: 0131-654 2774
e-mail: info@edinburgh-butterfly-world.co.uk
www.edinburgh-butterfly-world.co.uk**

Butterfly & Insect World
It's a jungle in here!

READERS' OFFER 2009

*£1.50 OFF full adult admission (max. 2 adults per voucher)
Photocopies not accepted. Valid during 2009.*

NOT TO BE USED IN CONJUNCTION WITH ANY OTHER OFFER

A fantastic display of gems, crystals, minerals and fossils. An experience you'll treasure forever. Gift shop, tearoom and AV display.

Open: Summer - 9.30am to 5.30pm daily; Winter - 10am to 4pm daily. Closed Christmas to end January.

Directions: follow signs from A75 Dumfries/Stranraer.

FHG GUIDES, ABBEY MILL BUSINESS CENTRE, PAISLEY PA1 1TJ • www.holidayguides.com

On show is a large collection, from 1899, of cars, bicycles, motor cycles and commercials. There is also a large collection of period advertising, posters and enamel signs.

Open: March-November - open daily 11am to 4pm. December-February - weekends 11am to 3pm or by special appointment.

Directions: off A198 near Aberlady. Two miles from A1.

FHG GUIDES, ABBEY MILL BUSINESS CENTRE, PAISLEY PA1 1TJ • www.holidayguides.com

Steam and heritage diesel passenger trains from Bo'ness to Birkhill for guided tours of Birkhill fireclay mines. Explore the history of Scotland's railways in the Scottish Railway Exhibition. Coffee shop and souvenir shop.

Open: weekends Easter to October, daily July and August.

Directions: in the town of Bo'ness. Leave M9 at Junction 3 or 5, then follow brown tourist signs.

FHG GUIDES, ABBEY MILL BUSINESS CENTRE, PAISLEY PA1 1TJ • www.holidayguides.com

See free-flying exotic butterflies in a tropical rainforest paradise. Have close encounters of the crawly kind in the 'Bugs & Beasties' exhibition that includes arrow frogs, tarantulas, amazing leaf-cutter ants and a unique seasonal Scottish Honey Bee display.

Open: daily. 9.30am-5.30pm summer, 10am-5pm winter.

Directions: located just off the Edinburgh City Bypass at the Gilmerton exit or at the Sherrifhall roundabout.

FHG GUIDES, ABBEY MILL BUSINESS CENTRE, PAISLEY PA1 1TJ • www.holidayguides.com

The story of Glasgow and the River Clyde brought vividly to life using AV, hands-on and interactive techniques. You can navigate your own ship, safely load your cargo, operate an engine, and go aboard the 130-year-old coaster 'Kyles'. Ideal for kids young and old wanting an exciting day out. New - The Clyde's Navy.

Open: 10am to 5.30pm daily

Directions: Green Car Park near M&S at Braehead Shopping Centre.

Award-winning attraction with unique 'Heather Story' exhibition, gallery, giftshop, large garden centre selling 300 different heathers, antique shop, children's play area and famous Clootie Dumpling restaurant.

Open: all year except Christmas Day and New Year's Day.

Directions: just off A95 between Aviemore and Grantown-on-Spey.

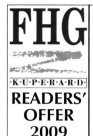

LLANBERIS LAKE RAILWAY

**Gilfach Ddu, Llanberis,
Gwynedd LL55 4TY
Tel: 01286 870549
e-mail: info@lake-railway.co.uk
www.lake-railway.co.uk**

READERS'
OFFER
2009

*One pet travels FREE with each full fare paying adult
Valid Easter to October 2009*

NOT TO BE USED IN CONJUNCTION WITH ANY OTHER OFFER

NATIONAL CYCLE COLLECTION

**Automobile Palace, Temple Street,
Llandrindod Wells, Powys LD1 5DL
Tel: 01597 825531
e-mail: cycle.museum@powys.org.uk
www.cyclemuseum.org.uk**

READERS'
OFFER
2009

*TWO for the price of ONE
Valid during 2009 except Special Event days*

NOT TO BE USED IN CONJUNCTION WITH ANY OTHER OFFER

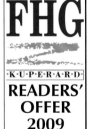

RHONDDA HERITAGE PARK

**Lewis Merthyr Colliery, Coed Cae Road,
Trehafod, Near Pontypridd CF37 2NP
Tel: 01443 682036
e-mail: info@rhonddaheritagepark.com
www.rhonddaheritagepark.com**

READERS'
OFFER
2009

*Two adults or children for the price of one when accompanied
by a full paying adult. Valid until end 2009 for full tours only.
Not valid on special event days/themed tours.*

NOT TO BE USED IN CONJUNCTION WITH ANY OTHER OFFER

Please note

All the information in this book is given in good faith in the belief that it is correct. However, the publishers cannot guarantee the facts given in these pages, neither are they responsible for changes in policy, ownership or terms that may take place after the date of going to press. Readers should always satisfy themselves that the facilities they require are available and that the terms, if quoted, still apply.

A 60-minute ride along the shores of beautiful Padarn Lake behind a quaint historic steam engine. Magnificent views of the mountains from lakeside picnic spots.

DOGS MUST BE KEPT ON LEAD AT ALL TIMES ON TRAIN

Open: most days Easter to October. Free timetable leaflet on request.

Directions: just off A4086 Caernarfon to Capel Curig road at Llanberis; follow 'Country Park' signs.

FHG GUIDES, ABBEY MILL BUSINESS CENTRE, PAISLEY PA1 1TJ • www.holidayguides.com

---

Journey through the lanes of cycle history and see bicycles from Boneshakers and Penny Farthings up to modern Raleigh cycles. Over 250 machines on display

PETS MUST BE KEPT ON LEADS

Open: 1st March to 1st November daily 10am onwards.

Directions: brown signs to car park. Town centre attraction.

FHG GUIDES, ABBEY MILL BUSINESS CENTRE, PAISLEY PA1 1TJ • www.holidayguides.com

---

Make a pit stop whatever the weather! Join an ex-miner on a tour of discovery, ride the cage to pit bottom and take a thrilling ride back to the surface. Multi-media presentations, period village street, children's adventure play area, restaurant and gift shop. Disabled access with assistance.

Open: Open daily 10am to 6pm (last tour 4pm). Closed Mondays Oct - Easter, also Dec 25th to early Jan.

Directions: Exit Junction 32 M4, signposted from A470 Pontypridd. Trehafod is located between Pontypridd and Porth.

FHG GUIDES, ABBEY MILL BUSINESS CENTRE, PAISLEY PA1 1TJ • www.holidayguides.com

Looking for holiday accommodation?

for details of hundreds of properties throughout the UK visit:

www.holidayguides.com

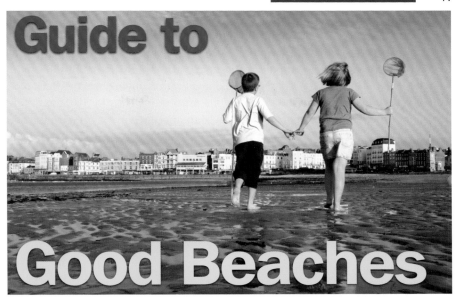

Guide to Good Beaches

How can I find a good, clean beach?
Can I take my dog on the beach?
How do I know the water is safe to swim in?

Britain has hundreds of beautiful beaches, many peaceful and secluded, others with lots of facilities which make them popular with families.

There are five beach scheme awards, and if you contact them or have a look at their websites, you will find lots of information on what is the best one for you and your family.

Started in 1987 as part of the EEC's Year of the Environment, the **BLUE FLAG** campaign aims not only to encourage and reward high standards of beach management at coastal resorts, but also to promote improved quality of bathing water. It is awarded in over 23 countries in Europe and South Africa for resort beaches and marinas with high standards of environmental management. To win a Blue Flag, therefore, water quality is judged along with cleanliness and beach facilities. A dog ban during the summer is an absolute requirement and only beaches regularly used by the public, and resorts with safe bathing all year round may enter the competition. In 2008 130 beaches in Britain were awarded the coveted Blue Flag Award. ENCAMS (Keep Britain Tidy Group) co-ordinates the scheme in England, while Keep Scotland Tidy, Keep Wales Tidy and Tidy Northern Ireland oversee the scheme in their respective countries.

ENCAMS (Environmental Campaigns) is a part-government funded charity working for the improvement of local environments. Its aims are to encourage individual, corporate and community responsibility for care of the environment through a variety of campaigns and programmes. All of the award-winning beaches have met very strict criteria, which include meeting the EC requirements for bathing water, providing good beach safety and supervision, putting in place good beach management (including dog controls and facilities for disabled visitors) and providing the public with clear information. A large database of UK beaches is maintained, with information on water quality, access, safety, cleanliness, dog control, first aid provision and conservation management.

 In England the **Encams Quality Coast Award** recognises different types of beach, and the website can be searched by region to find the perfect one for you.

In Scotland, Wales and Northern Ireland, Seaside Awards are presented annually for well maintained and managed resort and rural beaches, where bathing water quality must achieve the EC mandatory standard.

 Green Coast Award is run by Keep Wales Tidy and is given to unspoilt rural beaches in Wales and the Republic of Ireland for high water quality and best practice in environmental management. It places a great emphasis on community and environmental activities, and is intended to promote and protect rural beaches. Bathing water must achieve the EC Guideline standard.

The Marine Conservation Society produces a list of 'recommended' beaches which have the highest standards of bathing water quality. This award only addresses water quality and lists beaches which pose a minimum risk of sewage contamination and related diseases.

The Good Beach Guide (online www.goodbeachguide.co.uk) is a searchable database of 1200 beaches in the UK and Ireland, each with description, photo and map.

How to find out more:
Blue Flag Beaches • www.blueflag.org.uk
ENCAMS • www.encams.org
Seaside Awards • www.keepscotlandbeautiful.org
Green Coast Award • www.keepwalestidy.org
Marine Conservation Society • www.mcsuk.org

EUROPEAN
BLUE FLAG Beaches
in Britain and Northern Ireland
2008

Scotland
- Dundee & Angus
- Fife

Northern Ireland
- Londonderry
- Antrim
- Co. Down

North East England
- Tyne & Wear
- East Yorkshire
- North Yorkshire

Midlands
- Lincolnshire

Wales
- Anglesey
- Gwynedd
- North Wales
- Carmarthenshire
- Ceredigion
- Pembrokeshire
- South Wales

East England
- Norfolk
- Suffolk
- Essex

South West England
- Cornwall
- Dorset
- Devon

South East England
Hampshire • Kent • East Sussex • West Sussex • Isle of Wight

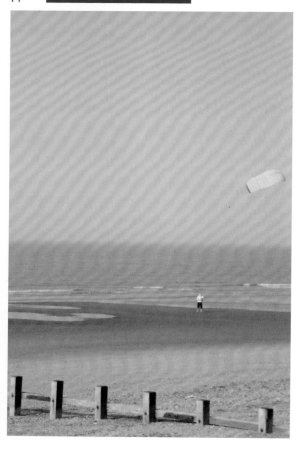

Dorset

Poole
  Canford Cliffs
  Branksome Chine
  Sandbanks
  Shore Road
Bournemouth
  Fisherman's Walk
  Alum Chine
  Durley Chine
  Southbourne
  Swanage Central

Hampshire

Hayling Island Central
Hayling Island West

Sussex

Hove Lawns
Eastbourne
Littlehampton Coastguards
West Wittering
West Street

Kent

Birchington Minnis Bay
Botany Bay
Herne Bay
Joss Bay
West Bay Westgate
St Mildred's Bay
Stone Bay, Broadstairs
Westbrook Margate
Tankerton
Ramsgate Main Sands
Margate Main Sands
Margate Walpole Bay

Isle of Wight

Sandown
Shanklin
Ventnor

Cornwall

Crooklets
Gyllyngvase
Porthtowan
Polzeath
Sennen Cove
Carbis Bay
Marazion
Porthmeor
Porthminster

North Devon

Woolacombe Sands
Westward Ho!
Ilfracombe Tunnels

South Devon

Bantham
Bigbury on Sea
Blackpool Sands
Challaborough
Dawlish Warren
Sandy Bay
Torbay
  Breakwater
  Broadsands
  Goodrington South
  Meadfoot
  Oddicombe
  Paignton Beach
  Preston Beach

Norfolk
Cromer
Mundesley
Sea Palling

Essex
Southend Jubilee Beach
Shoebury Common
Shoeburyness
Brightlingsea
Dovercourt

Suffolk
Felixstowe South
Lowestoft North
Lowestoft South
Southwold Pier

Lincolnshire
Mablethorpe Central
Skegness Central
Sutton on Sea Central

Tyne & Wear
Whitley Bay South
Tynemouth
  King Edwards Bay
  Longsands South
Sandhaven
Seaton Carew

East Yorkshire
Bridlington North
Hornsea
Withernsea

North Yorkshire
Scarborough North
Filey
Whitby

WALES

Gwynedd
Pwllheli
Fairbourne
Tywyn
Abersoch
Dinas Dinlle
Rhos-on-Sea/Colwyn Bay

Anglesey
Benllech
Church Bay
Llanddwyn
Porth Dafarch
Trearddur Bay

North Wales
Llandudno North Shore
Llandudno West Shore
Penmaenmawr
Prestatyn Central

Ceredigion
Borth
New Quay
Aberystwyth North
Aberystwyth South

Carmarthenshire
Pembrey Country Park
Pendine

Pembrokeshire
Dale
Broadhaven North
Lydstep
Newgale
Newport
Poppit Sands
Saundersfoot
St Davids Whitesands
Tenby Castle
Tenby North
Tenby South

South Wales
Porthcawl Rest Bay
Barry, Whitmore Bay
Port Eynon
Trecco Bay

SCOTLAND

Dundee & Angus
Montrose

Fife
Aberdour Silver Sands
Burntisland
Elie Harbour
Leven East
St Andrews West

NORTHERN IRELAND

Cranfield
Downhill
Magilligan/Benone Strand
Portrush West
Portrush White Rocks
Portstewart
Tyrella

Please note

All the information in this book is given in good faith in the belief that it is correct. However, the publishers cannot guarantee the facts given in these pages, neither are they responsible for changes in policy, ownership or terms that may take place after the date of going to press. Readers should always satisfy themselves that the facilities they require are available and that the terms, if quoted, still apply.

CORNWALL

Best Beaches

Several beaches which meet the strict criteria of the European Foundation for Environmental Education have been awarded a prestigious Blue Flag.

BLUE FLAG BEACHES 2008
- *Polzeath*
- *Carbis Bay*
- *Crooklets*
- *Marazion*
- *St Ives Porthmeor*
- *St Ives Porthminster*
- *Sennen Cove*
- *Gyllyngvase*
- *Porthtowan*

i **South West Tourism**
(Bristol & Bath, Cornwall, Devon, Dorset, Gloucestershire & The Cotswolds, Somerset, Wiltshire).
- **Tel: 0870 442 0880**
- **Fax: 0870 442 0881**
- **e-mail: post@swtourism.co.uk**
- **www.visitsouthwest.co.uk**

For more information about holidaying in Cornwall see:
- www.cornwalltouristboard.co.uk • 01872 322900
- www.cata.co.uk (Cornwall Association of Tourist Attractions)
- www.secta.org.uk (South East Cornwall)
- www.northcornwall-live.com (North Cornwall)
- www.go-cornwall.com (West Cornwall)

BUDE

⚓ **Family Fun Activities:** Seawater swimming pool on Summerleaze beach • Tropical Leisure Pool, including flume and wave machine, fitness suite, 10-pin bowling, roller blading rink and indoor adventure play area • Adventure centres offering tuition in various sports • Sports hall, multi-gym and activities • Sustrans cycle route • Bude Canal Wharf area • Heritage Trail • Museum • Mini-golf, putting, golf, bowls, squash, table tennis, cricket, tennis, sea and canal angling.

☆ **Special Events: May:** Model Boat Festival; re-enactment of Battle of Stamford Hill. **May-September:** events, shows, fetes and revels. **July:** Bude festival of Music, Downhill Classic Triathlon. **August:** arts & crafts exhibitions; Bude Carnival Week; Lifeboat Week; 8-day Bude Jazz Festival. **September:** Quadrathon. **October:** canoe sprint.

ℹ️ **Bude Visitor Centre, The Crescent, Bude EX23 8LE • 01288 354240 e-mail: budetic@visitbude.info www.visitbude.info**

⚓ Beaches

• **SUMMERLEAZE BEACH.** Level access via car park. *Safety and maintenance:* lifeguards during summer months. *Beach facilities:* beach huts, deck chairs etc for hire; mini-golf and go karts; open sea pool; cafe, shop and restaurant; RNLI centre/shop. Toilets, ♿ access. *Dog restrictions:* none, but they must be kept under proper control.

• **CROOKLETS BEACH.** Sandy, with level access. Car park adjoining. *Safety and maintenance:* lifeguards on duty during June/July/August. *Beach facilities:* deckchairs, beach huts, windbreaks etc for hire; snack bar and beach shop; toilets (disabled facilities for members of National Radar Key Scheme). *Dog restrictions:* banned from beach area from Good Friday to 1st October.

• **SANDY MOUTH BEACH.** Beach owned by National Trust. *Safety and maintenance:* lifeguards during summer months. *Beach facilities:* cafe owned by NT. Toilets but no ♿ facilities. *Dog restrictions:* none.

NEWQUAY

⚓ **Family Fun Activities:** Tunnels Through Time • Dairyland • Cornwall Pearl • Trerice Manor • Trenance Park with Water World fun pool and Newquay Zoo • Blue Reef Aquarium • Tennis, golf, pitch and putt, miniature railway, lakeside cafe, boating, sailing, surfing (Fistral Beach), angling, golf course • Discos, nightclubs.

☆ **Special Events: June:** Newquay Surf Triathlon. **July:** Surf Festival, Newquay Harbour Sports. **August:** British Surfing Championships. Gig racing.

ℹ️ **Tourist Information Centre, Marcus Hill, Newquay • 01637 854020 www.newquay.org.uk**

⚓ Beaches

• **HARBOUR BEACH.** Sandy and naturally sheltered; promenade and limited parking. *Safety and maintenance:* cleaned daily. *Beach facilities:* pleasure craft; fishing and shark trips; ice cream kiosk; restaurant; toilets with ♿ access.

• **TOWAN BEACH.** 400 yards long, sandy with rock pools, naturally sheltered promenade. ♿ access. Parking 5 minutes' walk. *Safety and maintenance:* flagged, warning signs, lifeguards; cleaned daily. *Beach facilities:* deck chairs, windbreaks, wet suits; ice-cream kiosk, snack bar.

• **GREAT WESTERN BEACH.** 200 yards long, sandy with rock pools and cliffs; parking 5 minutes' walk. *Safety and maintenance:* flagged, warning signs, lifeguards; cleaned daily. *Beach facilities:* deck chairs, windbreaks, surfboards; ice cream and snack bar; toilets with ♿ access.

- **TOLCARNE BEACH.** 500 yards long, sandy. Access down cliff steps, also path to beach. Parking 6 minutes' walk. *Safety and maintenance:* flagged, warning signs; cleaned daily. *Beach facilities:* deck chairs, surfboards, beach huts, trampolines; ice-cream kiosks, cafeteria, beach shop, barbecues; toilets.

- **LUSTY GLAZE BEACH.** 200 yards long; sandy with cliffs and rock pools, access via steps. *Safety and maintenance:* flagged, warning signs, lifeguards; cleaned daily. *Beach facilities:* deck chairs, surf boards, beach huts; ice-cream kiosk, cafe/takeaway, pub/restaurant and beach shop; showers and toilets; outdoor adventure centre. *Dog restrictions:* banned between 8am and 7pm.

- **PORTH BEACH.** 300 yards long, sandy and naturally sheltered with rock pools. Good parking. *Safety and maintenance:* flagged, warning signs, lifeguards; cleaned daily. *Beach facilities:* deck chairs, boogie boards, windbreaks; ice-cream kiosks, snack bars, restaurant and pub. *Dog restrictions:* banned from Easter to end September.

- **WHIPSIDERRY BEACH.** 200 yards long; sandy with cliffs and steps. *Safety and maintenance:* warning signs; cut off by tidal seas around cliffs.

- **WATERGATE BEACH.** Two miles long, sandy; good parking. *Safety and maintenance:* flagged, warning signs, lifeguards; cleaned daily. *Beach facilities:* surfboards; surf school and power kite school; bistro and takeaway, shops; toilets.

- **CRANTOCK BEACH.** Approx. one mile long, naturally sheltered with sandy dunes; good parking. *Safety and maintenance:* flagged, warning signs, lifeguards; Gannel tidal estuary very dangerous when tide going out. Beach owned and cleaned by NT. *Beach facilities:* deck chairs, surf boards; ice-cream kiosks, snack bars; toilets.

- **FISTRAL BEACH.** Approx. one mile long, sandy with dunes; good parking. *Safety and maintenance:* flagged, warning signs, lifeguards; cleaned daily. *Beach facilities:* deck chairs and windbreaks; wetsuit and surfboard hire; restaurant, cafe and takeaway, shops; toilets with & access.

PENZANCE

Family Fun Activities: Water sports area at Marazion • Sea water swimming pool, indoor swimming pool, children's playground, boating lake, amusement arcade • Riding, tennis, bowls, putting, go-karting • Shark fishing, sailing, sub-aqua, sea and fresh water angling • Rock climbing • Cinema, arts theatre, dance halls and discos, clubs and pub entertainment nightly.

Special Events: April: British Funboard Cup, Hockey Festival. **June:** Golowan Festival. **August:** Newlyn Fish Festival. **September:** Michaelmas Fair.

Tourist Information Centre, Station Road, Penzance TR18 2NF
01736 362207
www.go-cornwall.com

ST IVES

Family Fun Activities: Boat trips, sea angling, sailing, surfing, parascending, tennis, bowling, squash, putting • Leisure centre with swimming pool and gym • Museum, art galleries (Tate St Ives).

Tourist Information Centre, The Guildhall, St Ives TR26 2DS
01736 796297
www.stives-cornwall.co.uk

Beaches

- **PORTHMEOR BEACH.** One km long, sand backed by low cliffs. Good surfing beach. Limited parking. *Safety and maintenance:* area for use of surfboards marked with buoys, lifeguards in summer months; cleaned daily during holiday season. *Beach facilities:* deck chairs, surf boards, beach huts for hire; boat trips around bay; beach shop and cafe on promenade; toilets. *Dog restrictions:* banned from Easter to 1st October.

The Padstow to Rock ferry, Cornwall

Penrose Burden
Holiday Cottages

St Breward, Bodmin, Cornwall PL30 4LZ
Tel: 01208 850277 / 850617 • Fax: 01208 850915

Penrose Burden is the perfect place to relax, unwind and leave behind the pressures of modern life. Situated in North Cornwall and perched on the very edge of the majestic Bodmin Moor, which extends to over 100 square miles, it is surely one of the last completely unspoilt places in England. Its central location makes both coastlines easily accessible; the South with its long sandy beaches, historic ports, secluded creeks and the Eden Project, and the North with its dramatic cliffs, quiet coves, grand country houses and historic market towns.

Traditional stone buildings have been carefully converted to single level self-catering cottages and sympathetically designed with the needs of wheelchair users in mind. Exposed beams and original features blend well with walls hung with original paintings by local artists and simple modern furnishings. Each has a wood-burning stove with plentiful logs for year-round comfort, their own private garden, and outstanding views over our wooded valley and beyond to the dramatic moorland.

Easy access to some of the country's best surfing beaches, dinghy sailing, wind surfing, horse riding on the Moor, free salmon or trout fishing on our own mile of river bank, swimming and tennis (at the nearby country house hotel by arrangement), bike riding on The Camel Trail, or a game of golf on any one of the area's four golf courses.

...*just peace, tranquillity and space to relax*

Please write or telephone for a colour brochure.   Nancy Hall

www.penroseburden.co.uk

Visit the FHG website
www.holidayguides.com
for details of the wide choice of accommodation featured
in the full range of FHG titles

FHG Guides
publish a large range of well-known accommodation guides.
We will be happy to send you details or you can use
the order form at the back of this book.

Key to Symbols - see page 4
Please contact individual establishments to ensure that the facilities you require are available.

CORNWALL

Board

BUDE • Sunrise		*Terms on request*
🛏 7 🛁 7	BB ▥ 🪑 🐕	W Ⓐ ⊘
LIZARD PENINSULA • Polurrian Hotel		*B&B £56-£175 pppn*
🛏 39 🛁 39 ⟶ ✕ BB 🍴 ▥ 🪑 🔲 🐎 ⛰ 🐕	🍷 ⚲ ⚲ W	⊘
TRURO • Trenona Farm		*B&B £28-£40 pppn*
🛏 4 🛁 4	BB ▥ 🪑 🐕	W ⊘

CORNWALL

Self-catering

• **Classy Cottages**   *Terms on request*

BODMIN • **Penrose Burden Holiday Cottages**   *Terms on request*

BROADWOODWIDGER • **West Banbury Farm Cottages**   £250-£1230 *per week*

FALMOUTH • **Cornish Holiday Cottages**   £182-£2350 *per week*

FOWEY • **Penquite Farm**   *Terms on request*

FOWEY • **Fowey Harbour Cottages**   *Terms on request*

HAYLE • **St Ives Bay Holiday Park**   *Terms on request*

HOLYWELL BAY • **Trevornick Holiday Park**   *Terms on request*

LAUNCESTON • **Forget-me-Not Farm Holidays**   *Terms on request*

LAUNCESTON • **Bamham Farm Cottages**   £295-£1395 *per week*

LISKEARD • **Cutkive Wood Holiday Lodges**   *Terms on request*

LOOE • **Tremaine Green Country Cottages**   £190-£974 *per week*

MARAZION • **Trevarthian Holiday Homes**   £170-£840 *per week*

NEWQUAY • **Quarryfield Holiday Park**   *Terms on request*

SOUTH DEVON

 Best Beaches

As Britain's prime holiday area it is not surprising that South Devon is rich in fine beaches. Quality Coast Awards went to several beaches around this delightful coastline, where standards of cleanliness, safety and environmental management satisfied strict criteria.

ℹ️ **South West Tourism**

(Bristol & Bath, Cornwall, Devon, Dorset, Gloucestershire & The Cotswolds, Somerset, Wiltshire).

- **Tel: 0870 442 0880**
- **Fax: 0870 442 0881**
- **e-mail: post@swtourism.co.uk**
- **www.visitsouthwest.co.uk**

BLUE FLAG BEACHES 2008

- *Dawlish Warren*
- *Bantham*
- *Blackpool Sands*
- *Challaborough*
- *Bigbury-on-Sea*
- *Sandy Bay*
- *Torbay*
  Breakwater
  Goodrington Sands
  Meadfoot
  Oddicombe
  Broadsands
  Paignton Beach
  Preston Beach

For more information about holidaying in South Devon see:

- www.visitsouthdevon.co.uk
- www.southdevonaonb.org.uk (Area of Outstanding Natural Beauty)
- www.englishriviera.co.uk

EXMOUTH

Family Fun Activities: Indoor swimming pool, children's playground, boating lake, indoor sports centre, amusement arcade, mini-railway • Bowls, tennis, indoor tennis centre, putting, cricket, approach golf • Boat trips, angling • Old tyme and modern dancing,

Special Events: End July: Carnival events. **October:** Winter Floodlit Carnival.

i Tourist Information Centre, Alexandra Terrace, Exmouth EX8 INZ
Tel: 01395 222299
e-mail: info@exmouthtourism.co.uk
www.exmouthguide.co.uk

Beaches

• **MAER, RODNEY BAY AND EXMOUTH BEACH.** Beaches two-and-a-half miles long. Rodney Bay naturally sheltered, others open; promenade and good parking. *Safety and maintenance:* warning flags, lifeguards peak summer season; cleaned daily. *Beach facilities:* deck chairs, swings; beach huts for hire from T.I.C.; ice-cream kiosks, snack bars, restaurants and pubs; toilets with & access. *Dog restrictions:* banned from main beach from 1st May to 30th September.

PLYMOUTH

Family Fun Activities: Plymouth Pavilions with leisure pool, ice-skating, bar, bistro and shops • Mayflower Visitor Centre • National Marine Aquarium • Sports centre, indoor and outdoor swimming pools, parks with children's playgrounds • Tennis, putting, bowls, squash, dry-ski slope, bowling • Marina and water sports centre, sailing schools, sea angling • Theatre, multi-screen cinemas; museum and art gallery.

Special Events: May: Lord Mayor's Day Procession; Half Marathon, Vehicle and Bus Rally. **June:** Plymouth Playfair. **July:** Saltram Fair. **July:** World Championship Powerboat Race. **August:** National Fireworks Championships. **September:** Heritage Open Days. **November:** Christmas Lights.

i Tourist Information Centre, Plymouth Mayflower, The Barbican, Plymouth
Tel: 01752 306330
e-mail: barbicantic@plymouth.gov.uk
www.visitplymouth.co.uk

Beaches

• **BEACHES.** The city itself has an attractive waterfront with sheltered promenades and rock pools, and a fully restored Art Deco Lido. There are good parking facilities, toilets, ice-cream kiosks, snack bars, and family restaurants/pubs.

SIDMOUTH

Family Fun Activities: Children's playgrounds • Cricket, golf, angling, sailing, putting, tennis, bowls.

Special Events: August: International Folk Festival. **September:** Sidmouth Carnival.

i Tourist Information Centre, Ham Lane, Sidmouth • 01395 516441
e-mail: enquiries@sidmouth.co.uk
www.visitsidmouth.co.uk

Beaches

• **MAIN BEACH.** Half-a-mile long, shingle and sand at low tide; promenade and ample parking. *Safety and maintenance:* lifeguards present only on Sundays; cleaned daily. *Beach facilities:* beach huts, deck chairs; ice-cream kiosk; toilets with & access. *Dog restrictions:* banned from 1st May to 30th September.

TEIGNMOUTH & SHALDON

⚓ Family Fun Activities: Victorian Pier • Children's play area • Outdoor heated pool • Crazy golf • Bowls • Angling • Golf course • Summer shows.

☆ Special Events: June: Folk Festival. **July/August:** Summer Fun Fest. **July:** Carnival and Regatta. **August:** Water Carnival and Regatta. **November:** Jazz Festival, Winter Carnival.

i Tourist Information Centre, The Den, Teignmouth TQ14 8BE • 01626 215666 e-mail: teigntic@teignbridge.gov.uk www.southdevon.org.uk

⛱ Beaches

• **TEIGNMOUTH TOWN BEACH.** Long, sandy beach stretching from mouth of River Teign east towards Dawlish. *Safety and maintenance:* information signage, lifeguard patrol May-Sept; lifesaving equipment; daily beach cleaning. *Beach facilities:* deck chairs; beach wheelchair for hire; ice-cream kiosks and snack bars; toilets, showers; (♿ access to beach). *Dog restrictions:* not allowed on designated areas of the beach from 1st May to 30th Sept.

• **NESS BEACH, SHALDON.** Shingle beach sloping gently to the sea; safe bathing, rock pools at low tide No ♿ access. *Safety and maintenance:* lifesaving equipment, information signage; daily beach cleaning. *Beach facilities:* shops and toilets nearby. *Dog restrictions:* none.

FREE AND REDUCED RATE HOLIDAY VISITS!
Don't miss our
Readers' Offer Vouchers
on pages 9-40

DAWLISH

⚓ Family Fun Activities: Sports centre •Amusement arcades • Approach golf, putting, crazy golf, bowls • Angling • Theatre • Boat trips •Visitor Centre at Dawlish Warren Nature Reserve.

☆ Special Events: June: Arts Festival. **July/August:** Summer Fun Fest. **August:** Carnival.

i Tourist Information Centre, The Lawn, Dawlish EX7 9PW • 01626 215665 e-mail: dawtic@teignbridge.gov.uk www.southdevon.org.uk

⛱ Beaches

• **DAWLISH TOWN BEACH.** Mixture of sand and shingle, gently sloping to sea; safe family beach a short walk from town centre; poor ♿ access. *Safety and maintenance:* information signage, lifesaving equipment; cleaned daily. *Beach facilities:* deck chairs, ice-cream kiosks and snack bars; toilets with ♿ access. *Dog restrictions:* not allowed on designated areas of the beach from 1st May to 30th September.

• **CORYTON COVE.** Secluded, sandy beach within easy walking distance of town centre; ♿ access. *Safety and maintenance:* information signage, lifesaving equipment; cleaned daily. *Beach facilities:* beach hut hire, snack bar; toilets with ♿ access, showers. *Dog restrictions:* not allowed on designated areas of the beach from 1st May to 30th September.

• **DAWLISH WARREN.** Golden sands backed by sand dunes; easy access from main roads, good public transport links; ♿ access. *Safety and maintenance:* information signage, lifeguards May to September, lifesaving equipment; cleaned daily. *Beach facilities:* deck chairs; ice-cream kiosks and snack bars; toilets with ♿ access, showers. *Dog restrictions:* not allowed from slipway to groyne from 1st April to 30th September.

TORQUAY

⚓ **Family Fun Activities:** Windsurfing, sailing, angling • Indoor pools • Crazy golf, putting, tennis, squash, ten-pin bowling • Cinema, theatres, nightclubs, casino • Riviera Leisure Centre, museum, Babbacombe Model Village, cliff railway, Living Coasts.

☆ **Special Events:** **August:** Torbay Royal Regatta.

i **The Tourist Information Centre, Vaughan Parade, Torquay TQ2 5JG Tel: 01803 211211 e-mail: holiday@torbay.gov.uk www.englishriviera.co.uk**

🏖 Beaches

• **TORRE ABBEY SANDS.** 600 yards long, sandy and naturally sheltered; ♿ easy access, ample parking nearby. *Safety and maintenance:* warning flags, lifesaving equipment. *Beach facilities:* cafe/ refreshments; toilets nearby. *Dog restrictions:* dogs banned.

• **ANSTEY'S COVE.** 220 yards long, rock and shingle. Access steep in places. Parking 10 minutes' walk. *Safety and maintenance:* warning flags, lifesaving equipment. *Beach facilities:* refreshments, beach shop; toilets nearby. *Dog restrictions:* dogs allowed.

• **MEADFOOT BEACH.** 350 yards long, pebble and sand; easy access and ample parking. *Safety and maintenance:* lifesaving equipment. Lost Child centre. *Beach facilities:* cafe/ refreshments; toilets with baby changing facilities. *Dog restrictions:* allowed (Kilmorlie end).

• **ODDICOMBE BEACH.** 400 yards long, sand and shingle; access via clifflift. Parking 15 minutes' walk. *Safety and maintenance:* warning flags, lifesaving equipment, first aid post. *Beach facilities:* deck chair/sunbed hire; beach cafe/refreshments, beach shop; toilets with ♿ access and baby changing facilities. *Dog restrictions:* banned.

PAIGNTON

⚓ **Family Fun Activities:** Pier • Quay West water park and beach resort • Steam railway, amusement arcade, zoo, leisure centre with swimming pool • Boat trips, angling • Squash, badminton, tennis, putting, golf, go karting • Multiplex cinema, theatre.

☆ **Special Events:** **July:** Torbay Carnival. **August:** Paignton Regatta, Children's Festival.

i **Paignton TIC, Esplanade Road, Paignton TQ4 6ED • Tel: 01803 211211 e-mail: holiday@torbay.gov.uk www.englishriviera.co.uk**

🏖 Beaches

• **BROADSANDS BEACH.** Sandy beach, one-and-a-half miles long; easy access and ample parking. *Safety and maintenance:* warning flags, life-saving equipment, first aid post. *Beach facilities:* deck chair/chalet hire; refreshments, beach shop; toilets with ♿ access. *Dog restrictions:* banned.

• **GOODRINGTON SANDS.** 1200 yards long, sandy; ample parking. *Safety and maintenance:* warning flags. Lost Child centre. Patrol boat in operation. *Beach facilities:* deck chair/sunbed hire; cafe/ refreshments and restaurant, beach shop; toilets with ♿ access. *Dog restrictions:* banned on South Sands, allowed on North Sands.

• **PAIGNTON SANDS.** Sandy with rock pools, 1200 yards long; promenade and pier with arcades. *Safety and maintenance:* warning flags, life-saving equipment, first aid post. Lost Child centre. *Beach facilities:* deck chair/ sunbed hire; cafe/refreshments, restaurant, beach shop; toilets with ♿ access. *Dog restrictions:* banned.

• **PRESTON SANDS.** 600 yards long, sandy and naturally sheltered. *Safety and maintenance:* warning flags, life-saving equipment. *Beach facilities:* deck chair/ sunbed/chalet hire; cafe/refreshments, beach shop; toilets (toilets with ♿ access nearby). *Dog restrictions:* banned.

BRIXHAM

⌘ Family Fun Activities: Indoor and outdoor swimming pools • Tennis, squash, mini-golf, putting, leisure centre • Fishing trips/cruises, sailing • Berry Head Country Park • Golden Hind replica, museums.

☆ Special Events: May: Heritage Festival. June: Brixham Trawler Race. July: Brixham Happnin!!. August: Brixham Regatta.

i **Brixham T.I.C., Old Market House, The Quay, Brixham TQ5 8AW
Tel: 01803 211211
e-mail: holiday@torbay.gov.uk
www.englishriviera.co.uk**

⚓ Beaches

• **BREAKWATER BEACH.** Shingle beach, 100 yards long; easy access and ample parking; ♿ access difficult. *Safety and maintenance:* warning flags, life-saving equipment. *Beach facilities:* deck chairs; cafe/refreshments and restaurant; toilets. *Dog restrictions:* banned.

• **SHOALSTONE BEACH.** Shingle, with rock pools and sea water swimming pool; ♿ access difficult. *Safety and maintenance:* warning flags, lifeguards, life-saving equipment. *Beach facilities:* deck chair/ sunbed hire; cafe; toilets with baby changing facilities. *Dog restrictions:* banned from sea water swimming pool

• **ST MARY'S BAY.** Sand and shingle, parking 10 minutes' walk; ♿ access difficult. *Safety and maintenance:* swimming safe with care. *Dog restrictions:* allowed.

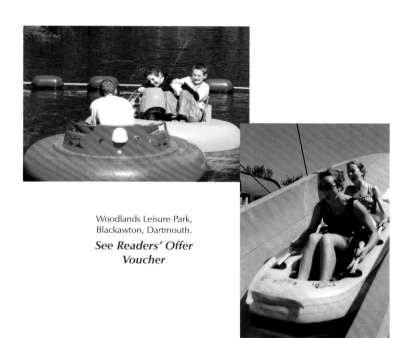

Woodlands Leisure Park, Blackawton, Dartmouth.

See Readers' Offer Voucher

☆ Fun for all the Family ☆

◆ **Babbacombe Model Village (01803 315315).** Masterpiece of miniature landscaping - hundreds of models and figures. www.babbacombemodelvillage.co.uk

◆ **Bickleigh Castle, near Tiverton (01884 855363).** Medieval romantic home with armoury, thatched Jacobean wing, early Norman chapel, moat and gardens.

◆ **Dartmoor Wildlife Park, Sparkwell (01752 837645).** Over 100 animals ranging from tigers, bears and wolves to birds of prey and even guinea pigs.

◆ **Kent's Cavern Show Caves, Torquay (01803 215136).** Stalactite caves of great beauty. Guided tours to discover the magic of Britain's earliest known settlement. www.kents-cavern.co.uk

◆ **National Marine Aquarium, Plymouth (01752 600301).** New attraction where memorable sights include a wall of ocean 15 metres wide and a shark theatre in over 700,000 litres of water. www.nationalaquarium.co.uk

◆ **Pennywell Farm & Wildlife Centre, Buckfastleigh (01364 642023).** A unique Devon family day out with hands-on activities and crafts. Ponies and piglets, quad bikes and train rides - there's always something going on. www.pennywellfarmcentre.co.uk

◆ **Paignton Zoo (01803 697500).** Over 300 species in spacious landscaped enclosures. Miniature railway, restaurant, activity centre. www.paigntonzoo.org.uk

◆ **Paignton and Dartmouth Steam Railway (01803 555872).** Seven-mile trip along the spectacular Torbay coast; gift shop, buffet. www.paignton-steamrailway.co.uk

◆ **River Dart Country Park, Ashburton (01364 652511).** Country fun for everyone - children's adventure playgrounds, nature trails, picnic meadow. www.dartmoor.co.uk

◆ **Sorley Tunnel Adventure Park, Kingsbridge (01548 854078).** A great all-weather day out, including Adventure World, Alien Play Planet, Equestrian World, Farm World - something for everyone.

◆ **South Devon Railway, Buckfastleigh (0845 345 1420).** Excursion trips on steam trains; museum, picnic area and play area. www.southdevonrailway.org

◆ **Woodlands Leisure Park, Dartmouth (01803 712598).** Lots of family fun activities, indoor and outdoor, plus hundreds of animals and birds. www.woodlands-leisure-park.co.uk

Standing in four acres of mature subtropical gardens, overlooking two miles of sandy beach, yet within easy reach of Dartmoor and Exeter, Devoncourt provides an ideal base for a family holiday.

BEDROOMS: The accommodation is in 52 single, double or family rooms, all with private bathroom, colour TV, tea and coffee making facilities and telephone.

LEISURE: Swimming pool, sauna, steam room, whirlpool spa, solarium and fitness centre, snooker room, hair and beauty salon. For those who prefer to be out of doors there is a tennis court, croquet lawn, attractive outdoor heated pool, 18 hole putting green and golf practice area, all within the grounds.

DINING: Attractive lounge bar and restaurant overlooking the fabulous gardens, with fantastic sea views from the large picture windows. Children's menus and vegetarian options available.

DEVONCOURT HOTEL Douglas Avenue, Exmouth, Devon EX8 2EX
Tel: 01395 272277 • Fax: 01395 269315
e-mail: enquiries@devoncourt.com • www.devoncourt.com

Aveland House

Aveland Road, Babbacombe,
Torquay, Devon, TQ1 3PT.
Tel: 01803 326622
Fax: 01803 328940
e-mail avelandhouse@aol.com
www.avelandhouse.co.uk

Quietly situated close to Cary Park and St Marychurch Village, just a short walk to Babbacombe sea front, beaches, shops, restaurants, theatres and attractions. Ideal location for holidays and short breaks.

- Green Tourism Gold Award
- Licensed
- All rooms en-suite
- Special diets catered for
- Free wi-fi internet access
- Car Park and Garden
- Non Smoking
- All major credit cards accepted

Rates from £30 B&B per person per night

Detached cottage, carefully renovated, retaining the inglenook fireplace, oak beams, floors and doors. Oil-fired central heating, colour TV, fully-equipped all-electric kitchen. Furnished to a high standard, sleeps six plus cot. Children and pets are welcome. Walled garden and garage. The villages and surrounding countryside are beautiful on the borders of Devon, Dorset, and Somerset. Many seaside towns within 10 miles – Lyme Regis, Charmouth and Seaton.

Lilac Cottage

Contact: **Mrs J. M. Stuart,**
2 Sandford House, Kingsclere,
Newbury, Berkshire RG20 4PA
Tel & Fax: 01635 291942
Mobile: 07787 550 413
e-mail: joanna.sb@free.fr

Smallridge,
Axminster, Devon

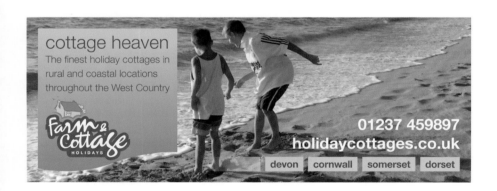
Visit the FHG website
www.holidayguides.com
for details of the wide choice of accommodation featured in the full range of FHG titles

A quiet, family-run park with 68 modern and luxury caravans for hire. The park overlooks the delightful River Axe Valley, and is just a 10 minute walk from the town with its wonderfully long, award-winning beach. Children will love our extensive play area, with its sand pit, paddling pool, swings and slide. Laundry facilities are provided and there is a wide selection of goods on sale in the park shop which is open every day. All of our caravans have a shower, toilet, fridge and TV. Also, with no clubhouse, a relaxing atmosphere is ensured. Prices from £90 per week; reductions for three or fewer persons early/late season.

Axevale Caravan Park
Colyford Road, Seaton, Devon EX12 2DF
Tel: 0800 0688816
e-mail: info@axevale.co.uk
www.axevale.co.uk

Cofton Country HOLIDAYS

Superb family-run four star holiday park in a Glorious Corner of Devon

• swimming pools • Swan pub • play areas • fishing lakes
• blue flag beach five minutes • take-away • park shop • WiFi
• holiday homes • touring • camping • cottages • apartments

0800 085 8649   www.coftonholidays.co.uk

FHG Guides

publish a large range of well-known accommodation guides.
We will be happy to send you details or you can use
the order form at the back of this book.

Key to Symbols - see page 4
Please contact individual establishments to ensure that the facilities you require are available.

SOUTH DEVON   Board

EXMOUTH • Devoncourt Hotel   *Terms on request*

🛏 52 🛏 52   ✕ BB ⛄ ▥ ⚲   ⚙   ⚱ ⌇ ⟿

TORQUAY • Aveland House   *B&B £30-£38pppn*

🛏 10 🛏 10   ⛟ ✕ BB ⛄ ▥ ⚲   ⚱   Ⓦ Ⓐ ⊘

SOUTH DEVON   Self-catering

• Farm & Cottage Holidays   *Terms on request*

⌂   ⊡ ⊞   ▥   🎠 ⚙ 🐕 ⚿ ⚱   Ⓐ

ASHBURTON • Parkers Farm Cottages & Caravans   *Terms on request*

🚐   ⌂   ⊞ ⛓ ▥ ⚲ 🎠 ⚙ 🐕 ⚿ ⚱

AXMINSTER • Lilac Cottage   *Terms on request*

⌂   ▥   🐕

BRIXHAM • Devoncourt Holiday Flats   *Terms on request*

🏘   ▥ ⚲   🐕   Ⓐ

DAWLISH WARREN • Cofton Country Holidays   *Terms on request*

🏘 🚐   ⌂   ⊡   ⛓ ▥ ⚲   ⚙   ⚿ ⚱   ⟿   Ⓐ

KINGSBRIDGE • Alston Farm Caravan & Camping Site   *Terms on request*

⛓   ⚙ 🐕

SEATON • Axevale Caravan Park   *£90-£550 per week*

🚐   ⊞ ⛓ ▥ ⚲   ⚙ 🐕   Ⓦ

for details of hundreds of properties throughout the UK visit:

www.holidayguides.com

NORTH DEVON

🏖 Best Beaches 🏖

Along with two other fine beaches from the area, Woolacombe Beach is once again a proud winner of a European Blue Flag, indicating strict beach management and the highest standard of bathing water under EC legislation. Quality Coast Awards also went to beaches in this area.

BLUE FLAG BEACHES 2008
- *Ilfracombe (Tunnels)*
- *Westward Ho!*
- *Woolacombe*

 South West Tourism
(Bristol & Bath, Cornwall, Devon, Dorset, Gloucestershire & The Cotswolds, Somerset, Wiltshire).
- **Tel: 0870 442 0880**
- **Fax: 0870 442 0881**
- **e-mail: post@swtourism.co.uk**
- **www.visitsouthwest.co.uk**

FREE AND REDUCED RATE HOLIDAY VISITS!
Don't miss our Readers' Offer Vouchers on pages 9-40

For more information about holidaying in North Devon see:
- www.northdevon.com
- www.northdevon-aonb.org.uk (Area of Outstanding Natural Beauty)
- www.visit-exmoor.co.uk

LYNTON & LYNMOUTH

Family Fun Activities: Children's playgrounds • Putting, tennis, bowls, cricket, horse riding • Boat trips, river and sea fishing • Cinema • Brass rubbing, museum • Local crafts centre • Unique water-operated cliff railway linking twin resorts.

i Tourist Information Centre, Town Hall, Lynton
0845 660 3232 • Fax: 01598 752755
e-mail: info@lyntourism.co.uk
www.lyntourism.co.uk

Beaches

• **LEE BAY BEACH.** Half-a-mile long, sand and shingle, with access through Valley of Rocks and on to Lee Abbey bottom lodge (toll charge); parking in field overlooking sea. *Safety and maintenance:* safe within the bay, cleaned whenever necessary. *Beach facilities:* refreshments five minutes' walk (restricted opening), toilets two minutes' walk. *Dog restrictions:* banned.

• **LYNMOUTH BEACH.** Large rocky beach, long slipway, Rhenish tower guarding harbour. *Safety and maintenance:* safe within the bay, cleaned whenever necessary. *Dog restrictions:* none .

ILFRACOMBE

Family Fun Activities: Heated indoor pool, children's playground, boating lake, go karting, sports canoes • Pier, angling • Tennis, putting, pitch and putt, crazy golf, golf course • Theatre with shows all year round, cinema, discos.

i Tourist Information Centre, The Promenade, Ilfracombe • 01271 863001
e-mail: info@ilfracombe-tourism.co.uk
www.ilfracombe-tourism.co.uk

☆ **Special Events: June:** Victorian Celebration. **July:** North Devon Arts Youth Festival. **August:** Emergency Rescue Service Display. **August/September:** Flower Shows.

Beaches

• **HARBOUR BEACH.** 200 yards long, sandy and naturally sheltered; good parking. Promenade, pier with arcade and cafe; toilets and parking. *Beach facilities:* ice-cream kiosks, snack bars, restaurants and pubs; toilets with &. access.

• **HELE BAY BEACH.** Half-a-mile long, shingle (some sand) with rock pools; promenade, good parking. *Safety and maintenance:* cleaned regularly during season. *Beach facilities:* deck chairs, sports canoes; ice-cream kiosk, snack bars, restaurants and pubs; toilets with &. access

• **LARKSTONE BEACH.** 100 yards long, shingle and rock pools, naturally sheltered; good parking. *Safety and maintenance:* cleaned regularly in season. *Beach facilities:* ice-cream kiosk; toilets with &. access.

• **RAPPAREE BEACH.** 220 yards long, shingle with rock pools and cliffs, naturally sheltered; promenade, good parking. *Safety and maintenance:* warning signs; certain parts cut off at high tide; cleaned regularly during season.

- **TUNNELS BEACHES.** 600 yards long, shingle with rock pools and cliffs; naturally sheltered, good parking. *Safety and maintenance:* warning signs, certain parts cut off at high tide; beach privately owned and cleaned daily during season. *Beach facilities:* deck chairs, sports canoes, rowing boats; ice-cream kiosk and snack bar; toilets.

- **WHITE PEBBLE BEACH.** 220 yards long, shingle and pebbles. Cliffs, naturally sheltered; parking. *Safety and maintenance:* warning signs, certain parts cut off at high tide.

- **WILDERSMOUTH BEACH.** 220 yards long, shingle with rock pools; naturally sheltered; promenade, good parking. *Safety and maintenance:* cleaned by Local Authority. *Beach facilities:* deck chairs; ice-cream kiosks, snack bars, restaurants and pubs; ramps with ♿ access.

WOOLACOMBE

Family Fun Activities: Repertory theatre and other entertainment in season.

Special Events: July: Grand Sandcastle Competition. **September:** National Surf Life Saving Championships (every 3rd year). Other surf and water competitions during year.

[i] Tourist Information Centre, The Esplanade, Woolacombe EX34 7DL • 01271 870553 e-mail: info@woolacombetourism.co.uk www.woolacombetourism.co.uk

Beaches

WOOLACOMBE SANDS BEACH. 3 miles long, sandy and naturally sheltered; good parking. *Safety and maintenance:* flagged, warning signs, lifeguards (May to September); cleaned daily. *Beach facilities* (May to September): deck chairs, beach huts, children's amusements, ice-cream kiosks, snack bars, restaurants and pubs; toilets with ♿ access. *Dog restrictions:* some restricted areas in operation May to September. Blue Flag and Seaside Award since 1991. England for Excellence Award for Best Family Holiday 1999.

☆ Fun for all the Family ☆

◆ **Arlington Court (NT), Barnstaple (01271 850296).** A fascinating collection including shells and model ships. Surrounding park has Shetland ponies and a flock of Jacob's sheep. Teas and snacks.

◆ **The Big Sheep, Abbotsham (01237 472366).** All you ever wanted to know about sheep – lots of lambs, plus sheep dairy, shearing, sheepdog trials. Ewetopia indoor playground. Shop and restaurant.
www.thebigsheep.co.uk

◆ **Gnome Reserve, Near Bradworthy (01409 241435).** For the young at heart - from 1 to 101! Four acres of woodland, meadow and garden is home to over 1000 gnomes and pixies. Gnome hats loaned free of charge to make you feel at home!
www.gnomereserve.co.uk

◆ **Combe Martin Wildlife and Dinosaur Park (01271 882486).** Otters, falcons, nature walks, children's playground and zoo, large indoor model railway.
www.dinosaur-park.com

◆ **Dartington Crystal, Torrington (01805 626244).** Marvel at the glass-blower's skill and trace the development of manufacturing techniques over the centuries. Factory shop and restaurant.
www.dartington.co.uk

◆ **Escot Park, Ottery St Mary (01404 822188).** Enjoy the gardens and fantasy woodland which surround this historic house. Maze, aquatic and pet centre, craft and gift shop - a place fop people who love Nature.
www.escot-devon.co.uk

◆ **Exmoor Zoological Park, Bratton Fleming (01598 763352).** Formal and natural gardens with a large collection of tropical birds. Tarzanland for children; tearoom and gift shop.
www.exmoorzoo.co.uk

◆ **Jungleland, Barnstaple (01271 343884).** Collection of plants from all over the world in near as possible natural settings.

◆ **The Milky Way, Clovelly (01237 431255).** Hand milk a cow, bottle feed lambs, goats and calves. Adventure playground and old farm machinery.
www.themilkyway.co.uk

◆ **Once Upon A Time, Woolacombe (01271 870900).** Children's park with train rides, adventure trails, soft play area.

◆ **Rosemoor Garden, Great Torrington (01805 624067).** Garden (now RHS) started in 1959: rhododendrons, ornamental trees and shrubs, primulas, young arboretum.
www.rhs.org.uk/gardens/rosemoor

See the Family-Friendly Pubs & Inns
Supplement on pages 178-181 for establishments
which really welcome children

fun filled holidays

four award winning Holiday Parks set in Devon's breathtaking countryside next to Woolacombe's 3 miles of golden Blue flag sandy beach! Safe friendly & fun, perfect for families

15% off* BABY BREAKS
for under 3's
- Special Baby Friendly Accommodation
- FREE Baby Beachball Pack
- FREE Baby Hand and footprint at Waves Ceramic Studio
- Complimentary Bottle of Wine and Spa Session for Parents

Special Deals for Kids Under 5 & Lone Parent Deals too

Kids cabaret & Entertainment

Face Painting, Party Dances & Fancy Dress Theme Nights

Billy Beachball Club (FREE) for 5-12 year olds!

Baby Break Discounts!

Billy Buddy Club (FREE) for kids Under 5!

I'll be at the Kids Clubs See you there!

SEAVIEW Holiday Homes & Luxury Lodges plus great Camping & Touring

over 40 FREE activities...
- 10 Heated Indoor & Outdoor Pools
- Waterslides • Health Suite • Cinema
- Nightly Entertainment & Star Cabaret
- Tennis • Snooker • Crazy Golf • Kid's Clubs
- Kid's Indoor & Outdoor Play Areas • Playzone
- Coarse Fishing Ponds ... Plus so much more!

...and for just a little more
- 10 Pin Bowling
- 17th Century Inn
- Waves Ceramic Studio
- Affiliated Golf Club
- Indoor Bowls Rinks
- WaterWalkerz
- Restaurants & Bars
- Activities Programme
- Kiddy Karts
- Sports Bar
- Amusement Arcade
- Beauty Salon
- Pirate Ship
- Bungee Run
- Climbing Wall
- Swimming Lessons

REGISTER ONLINE FOR LATEST OFFERS!!
woolacombe.com/fcw
01271 870 343

WOOLACOMBE BAY

*Baby Break discounts available all year excluding arrivals July 24 to Aug 28, 2009. T's & C's apply.

Key to Symbols - see page 4
Please contact individual establishments to ensure that the facilities you require are available.

NORTH DEVON
Board

BERRYNARBOR • Sandy Cove Hotel — *Terms on request*
🛏 39 🛁 39   ✕ BB   ▥ ⫟   🐕   ♟ 🔉

BIDEFORD • West Titchberry Farm — *Terms on request*
🛏 3 🛁 1   ✕ BB   🐎 ⚼

ILFRACOMBE • Wentworth House — *Terms on request*
🛏 10 🛁 8   ✕ BB   ▥ ⫟   ♟   Ⓐ ⊘

ILFRACOMBE • Strathmore — *B&B £33-£76 pppn*
🛏 8 🛁 8   BB   ▥ ⫟ ▣   🐕   ♟   W Ⓐ ⊘

OKEHAMPTON • Parsonage Farm — *Terms on request*
🛏 2 🛁 2   BB   🐎   ⊘

SOUTH MOLTON • Partridge Arms Farm — *B&B £25-£30 pppn*
🛏 7 🛁 5   🍼 ✕ BB 🍽 ▥ ⫟ ▣   ⚼ 🐕 ♿ ♟   ⊘

WOOLACOMBE • Woolacombe Bay Hotel — *B&B £80-£135pppn*
🛏 63 🛁 63   🍼 ✕ BB 🍽 ▥ ⫟ ▣ 🐎 ⚼   ♟ 🔉 🔉 W Ⓐ ⊘

NORTH DEVON
Self-catering

BARNSTAPLE• North Hill Cottages — *£195-£930 per week*
🏠   🗔   ▥ ⫟   ⚼ 🐕   🔉   Ⓐ

LITTLE TORRINGTON • Torridge House Farm Cottages — *Terms on request*
🏠   🗔   ▥ ⫟ 🐎 ⚼   🔉

SOUTH MOLTON • Partridge Arms Farm — *From £500 per week*
🗔 🗒   ▥ ⫟   ⚼ 🐕   Ⓐ

WOOLACOMBE • Woolacombe Bay Holiday Parks — *£100-£1100 per week*
🏨 🚐 🏡 🏠   🗔 🗒 ▦   🐎 ⚼ 🐕 ♿ ♟ 🔉 🔉 W

SOMERSET & WILTSHIRE

⛰ Best Beaches ⛰

There are some fine beaches in this delightful part of the country, including some of the West Country's most popular family holiday resorts. A Quality Coast Award has been gained once again by Burnham-on-Sea.

ⓘ **South West Tourism**
(Bristol & Bath, Cornwall, Devon, Dorset, Gloucestershire & The Cotswolds, Somerset, Wiltshire).

• **Tel: 0870 442 0880**
• **Fax: 0870 442 0881**
• **e-mail: post@swtourism.co.uk**
• **www.visitsouthwest.co.ukv**

FHG Guides
publish a large range of well-known accommodation guides.
We will be happy to send you details or you can use
the order form at the back of this book.

For more information about holidaying in Somerset see:
• www.visitsomerset.co.uk
• www.somersetcoast.com

For more information about holidaying in Wiltshire see:
• www.visitwiltshire.co.uk

MINEHEAD

Family Fun Activities: New look seafront with extensive sandy beach • Aquasplash Leisure Pool with wave machine • cruises and steam train rides • Horse riding and walking on nearby Exmoor • Theatre • Classic Car Collection • Butlins Family Entertainment Resort with a host of attractions including funfair, go karts, cinema, leisure pool and live shows.

☆ **Special Events: Late April/early May:** Hobby Horse festivities. **July:** Minehead and Exmoor Festival; Friends of Thomas the Tank Engine Weekend.

i Tourist Information Centre,
17 Friday Street, Minehead TA24 5UB
01643 702624 • Fax: 01643 707166
e-mail: mineheadtic@visit.org.uk
www.minehead.co.uk

Beaches

• **MINEHEAD STRAND BEACH.** Wide sandy beach with access down ramps from new sea wall. Ample parking. *Safety and maintenance:* cleaned daily. *Beach facilities:* cafe and takeaway food outlets; toilets with ♿ access. *Dog restrictions:* not allowed on beach from 1st May to 30th September; must be kept on lead on promenade.

• **MINEHEAD TERMINUS BEACH.** A mixture of sand and pebbles (continuation of the Strand in a westwards direction). *Facilities and Dog Restrictions:* as for Strand beach.

WESTON-SUPER-MARE

Family Fun Activities: The SeaQuarium • Grand Pier with amusements, land train, miniature railway, kids' play area • Marine lake • Donkey rides, amusements •Leisure centre • Tennis, putting, bowls, pitch and putt, ten-pin bowling, riding, rugby, football, cricket, fishing, golf • Cinema, museum, shows, night clubs, live music.

☆ **Special Events:** for a full up-to-date listing of events visit **www.visitsomerset.co.uk** or call the Tourist Information Centre. Events include national waterski races, Helidays, Sand Sculpture Festival, children's activities, Playhouse shows, motorcycle beach race and carnival.

i Tourist Information Centre, Beach Lawns, Weston-super-Mare BS23 1AT
Tel: 01934 888800
Minicom: 01934 643172
westontouristinfo@n-somerset.gov.uk
www.visitsomerset.co.uk

Beaches

• **BEACH.** Two miles long, sandy with rock pools and shingle at Anchor Head. Promenade and piers; good parking. *Safety and maintenance:* beach cleaned daily all year. *Beach facilities:* deck chairs, donkeys and pony carts, marine lake and fun castle; ice-cream kiosks, snack bars, restaurants and pubs; toilets, some with ♿ access. *Dog restrictions:* dog ban on section of main beach between May and September.

☆ Fun for all the Family ☆

◆ **Avon Valley Railway, near Bristol (0117 932 5538).** Working railway museum with locos and coaches. Enjoy a 5-mile trip along the lovely River Avon valley.
www.avonvalleyrailway.co.uk

◆ **Bee World and Animal Centre, Stogumber (01984 656545).** Unravel the mysteries of bee-keeping and meet lots of friendly animals at this unique "hands-on" centre. Children's play area.

◆ **Bristol Zoo (0117 974 7300).** Extensive and fascinating collection including pygmy hippos and gorillas. Over 300 species from lions to dung beetles.
www.bristolzoo.org.uk

◆ **Cheddar Caves & Gorge (01934 742343).** Famous for its caves and underground pools, in a deep winding fissure in the Mendip Hills. Exhibitions.
www.chedddarcaves.co.uk

◆ **Cholderton Rare Breeds Farm Park, near Salisbury** (01980 629438). Rare and endangered breeds of British farm animals, plus Rabbit World with over 50 varieties. Pig racing (Pork Stakes) in peak season.
www.choldertoncharliesfarm.com

◆ **Cricket St Thomas Wildlife Park, near Chard (01460 30111).** Large collection of wild animals and birds in 1000 acres of woodland and lakes.
www.cstwp.co.uk

◆ **Haynes Motor Museum, Sparkford, Near Yeovil (01963 440804).** Magnificent collection of over 250 vintage, veteran and classic cars, and 50 motorcycles. Experience 100 smiles per hour!
www.haynesmotormuseum.co.uk

◆ **Longleat Safari Park, Warminster (01985 844400).** 100-acre reserve for lions, giraffes, monkeys, zebras and tigers roaming free. World's longest hedge maze, Postman Pat village.
www.longleat.co.uk

◆ **Rode Bird Gardens, near Bath (01373 830326).** 17 acres of beautifully laid out grounds with hundreds of exquisitely coloured birds. Children's play area.

◆ **SS Great Britain, Bristol (0117 926 0680).** Splendid six-masted ocean going vessel dating from 1843 and associated with engineering genius Isambard Kingdom Brunel.
www.ss-great-britain.com

◆ **SeaQuarium, Weston-super-Mare (01934 613361).** Exciting close encounters with marvels of marine life, from starfish to sharks. Feeding demonstrations, talks and special presentations.
www.seaquarium.co.uk

◆ **STEAM - Museum of Great Western Railway, Swindon (01793 466646).** Fun hands-on exhibits and rare archive footage tell the story of this famous railway company.
www.steam-museum.org.uk

◆ **West Somerset Railway, Bishops Lydeard (01643 704996).** A nostalgic journey through the unspoilt beauty of the Quantock Hills and along the coast; Visitor Centre and model railway.
www.west-somerset-railway.co.uk

◆ **Wookey Hole, Wells (01749 672243).** Britain's most spectacular caves, with dramatic lighting effects. Also paper making demonstrations, Magical Mirror Maze.
www.wookey.co.uk

Mill Farm Caravan & Camping Park

**FIDDINGTON,
BRIDGWATER,
SOMERSET TA5 1JQ**

SWIMMING – TROPICAL INDOOR HEATED
POOLS AND TWO OUTDOOR POOLS WITH
GIANT WATER SLIDE ★ RIDING
★ BOATING ★ HOLIDAY APARTMENTS TO LET
Attractive, sheltered farm site. Between
beautiful Quantock Hills and the sea.
Boating, swings, table tennis, TV, tourist information, large sand pit.
FOR HIRE: Canoes, trampolines and ponies.
★ Club Entertainment ★ Caravan storage available.

CLEAN TOILETS ETC, LAUNDRY
ROOM, ELECTRIC HOOK-UPS,
CAMP SHOP, GOOD LOCAL PUBS.
OPEN ALL YEAR.

WRITE OR PHONE FOR BROCHURE

Tel: M. J. Evans:
01278 732286
www.millfarm.biz

FOXHANGERS CANALSIDE FARM
Lower Foxhangers, Rowde, Devizes SN10 1SS
Tel & Fax: 01380 828254
e-mail: sales@foxhangers.co.uk • www.foxhangers.com

Small farm/marina with its many diverse attractions situated alongside the famous "Caen Hill"
flights of 29 locks. Hear the near musical clatter of the windlass heralding the lock gate
opening and the arrival of yet another colourful narrowboat. Relax on the patios of our rural
retreats - four holiday mobile homes, all new models, sleeping 4/6. Ideally situated for fishing,
cycling or walking. Pubs within easy walking distance. Short breaks when available. Secluded
campsite nestling under the hedgerows, with electricity and facilities. Also narrowboat hire for
weekly or short breaks. Avebury, Stonehenge, Bath and Longleat all close by

Colin and Cynthia Fletcher

Key to Symbols - see page 4
Please contact individual establishments to ensure that the facilities you require are available.

SOMERSET & WILTSHIRE
Board

SALISBURY • Hayburn Wyke *Terms on request*
BB ▥ W Ⓐ ⊘

THEALE • Yew Tree Farm *Terms on request*
🛏 3 🛁 2 ✕ BB ⊔ 🐕 ♉

WESTBURY • Spinney Farmhouse *Terms on request*
🛏 3 ✕ BB 🐕 Ⓐ ⊘

WESTON-SUPER-MARE • Moorlands *B&B £25-£35 pppn*
🛏 6 🛁 4 👶 BB ⊔ ▥ 🪑 🐕 ♿ Ⓐ ⊘

SOMERSET & WILTSHIRE
Self-catering

BRIDGWATER • Mill Farm Caravan & Camping Park *Terms on request*
🏠 🧺 🎠 ⚊ 🏊 🚴 W Ⓐ

DEVIZES • Foxhangers Canalside Farm *£175-£415 per week*
🚐 🖼 ▥ 🪑 🐕 ⊘

MINEHEAD • St Audries Bay Holiday Club *Terms on request*
🚐 🏠 🧺 🎠 ⚊ ♉ 🏊

TAUNTON • Quantock Orchard Caravan Park *Terms on request*
🚐 🧺 🎠 ⚊ 🐕 🚴

WINSCOMBE • Home Farm Cottages *Terms on request*
🏠 🗐 ⚊ ⊘

FHG Guides
publish a large range of well-known accommodation guides.
We will be happy to send you details or you can use
the order form at the back of this book.

HAMPSHIRE & DORSET

 Best Beaches

No less than 11 beaches in the area have won European Blue Flag Awards for 2008.

BLUE FLAG BEACHES 2008

- *Bournemouth*
  Fisherman's Walk
  Alum Chine
  Durley Chine
  Southbourne
- *Poole*
  Canford Cliffs Chine
  Sandbanks
  Shore Road
  Branksome Chine
- *Swanage Central*
- *Hayling Island Central*
- *Hayling Island West*

i South East England Tourism
- **Tel: 023 8062 5400**
- **Fax: 023 8062 0010**
- **e-mail: enquiries@tourismse.com**
- **www.visitsoutheastengland.com**

i South West Tourism
(Bristol & Bath, Cornwall, Devon, Dorset, Gloucs & The Cotswolds, Somerset, Wiltshire).
- **Tel: 0870 442 0880**
- **Fax: 0870 442 0881**
- **e-mail: post@swtourism.co.uk**
- **www.visitsouthwest.co.uk**

For more information about holidaying in Dorset see:
- www.dorsetforyou.com
- www.westdorset.com (West Dorset)
- www.ruraldorset.com (North Dorset)
- www.dorset-newforest.com

For more information about holidaying in Hampshire see:
- www.vist-hampshire.co.uk

BOURNEMOUTH

⚓ Family Fun Activities: Seven miles

of golden sand, first-class attractions, beautiful gardens and summer festivals offer something for everyone from the Oceanarium to the Bournemouth International Centre and the Russell-Cotes Museum. There is plenty to do whatever the weather. Try the Bournemouth Eye tethered balloon ride.

Free 'Family Fun' brochure available on request from Visitor Information Bureau.

☆ Special Events: School Summer

Holidays: Kids Fun Festival with more than 100 free shows and activities. Sporting events, competitions and festivals take place throughout the year.

ⓘ **Visitor Information Bureau,**
Westover Road, Bournemouth BH1 2BU
Information line and accommodation
enquiries: 0845 0511700
e-mail: info@bournemouth.gov.uk
www.bournemouth.co.uk

⚒ Beaches

• **BEACH.** 7 miles long, sandy with traffic-free promenade, reached by zig-zag paths or cliff lifts. *Safety and maintenance:* lifeguard patrols, close-circuit TV surveillance, first-aid posts; cleaned twice daily. *Beach facilities:* children's beach GameZone in summer; rowing boats, pedalos, speed boats, kayaks, surfing; beach hut hire. "No Smoking" zones. Special 'Kidzone' safety areas. Excellent catering facilities. *Dog restrictions:* Dog-friendly sections of beach at Fisherman's Walk and Alum Chine between May and September inclusive; allowed on the promenade on lead.

POOLE

⚓ Family Fun Activities: Poole Quay

with shops, crafts, museums, Poole Pottery, restaurants • Crab lining, fishing trips, harbour boat trips, wind-surfing and sailing in Europe's largest natural harbour • Brownsea Island and road train • Poole Park with Gus Gorilla's indoor playground, crazy golf, Poole Park train, mini icerink • Sports centres with swimming, badminton, squash, etc • Tower Park Entertainment Centre with cinema, Bowlplex, Splashdown, restaurants • Monkey World • Poole Museum with free entry.

Free 'Family Fun' brochure available on request from Poole Tourist Office.

☆ Special Events: May/September:

programme of spectacular weekday events featuring motorcycles, car nostalgia, fireworks, speedway, live entertainment, children's activities. **September:** Animal Windfest.

ⓘ **Poole Welcome Centre, Poole Quay,**
Poole BH15 1HJ
01202 253253
e-mail: tourism@pooletourism.com
www.pooletourism.com

⚒ Beaches

• **BEACH.** Three miles of sands stretching from Sandbanks to Branksome Dene Chine. 7 car parks. *Safety and maintenance:* cleaned daily; lifeguard coverage in main season, beach station at Sandbanks manned throughout year. *Beach facilities:* beach huts, deckchairs and windbreaks for hire; watersports; ice-cream kiosks, snacks and cafe; toilets with ♿ facilities. *Dog restrictions:* banned from main beaches from May to September, must be kept on lead on promenade at all times.

A useful index of towns/counties appears on page 182

SWANAGE

⚏ Family Fun Activities:
Bowling green, tennis, putting, crazy golf, 18-hole pitch and putt course, trampolines • Swanage Bay View Restaurant • Holiday park with swimming pool, skittle alley, indoor bowls and trimnasium • Water ski-ing, windsurfing, sailing, motor boats, sea angling • Castle, lighthouse, country park • Theatre/cinema.

☆ Special Events:
July: Swanage Jazz Festival. **August:** Regatta and Carnival Week. **September:** Swanage Folk Festival

ⓘ Tourist Information Centre, Shore Road, Swanage BH19 1LB • 0870 4420680
e-mail: mail@swanage.gov.uk
www.swanage.gov.uk

🏖 Beaches

• **SWANAGE BAY BEACH.** Three miles long, sandy and naturally sheltered; promenade and good parking. *Safety and maintenance:* cleaned daily. *Beach facilities:* deck chairs, Punch and Judy; pedalcraft; toilets with ♿ facilities. *Dog restrictions:* banned from main beach from 1st May to 30th September; must be kept on lead on promenade.

WEYMOUTH

⚏ Family Fun Activities:
Country Park with Model World, Sea Life Park, Miniature Railway, Mini-Golf, Leisure Ranch and RSPB Nature Reserve • Weymouth Old Harbour including Brewers Quay Complex and Weymouth Timewalk, Sharky's, Nothe Fort and Gardens, Tudor House. • Pleasure cruises, float and boat hire, sailing, sub-aqua sports • Tennis, bowls • Swimming pool • Theatre with family shows, cinemas, night clubs • Superbowl

☆ Special Events:
May: Beach Kite Festival, Trawler Race and Water Carnival. **July/August:** Beach Volleyball Championships, Spirit of the Sea Festival. **August:** weekly Firework Festival, Weymouth Carnival. **October:** Beach Motocross.

ⓘ Tourist Information, King's Statue, Weymouth • 01305 785747
e-mail: tourism@weymouth.gov.uk
www.visitweymouth.co.uk

🏖 Beaches

• **WEYMOUTH BAY BEACH.** Two and a half miles long, sand running into shingle; promenade and piers. *Safety and maintenance:* Beach Control Centre, lifeguards; first aid and lost children post; beach cleaned daily. *Beach facilities:* donkey rides, deck chairs, Punch and Judy, trampolines, amusement arcades; floats, canoes; ice-cream kiosks, restaurants and pubs; toilets with ♿ facilities. *Dog restrictions:* dogs restricted to special areas May-September.

Sandbanks, Poole

☆ Fun for all the Family ☆

◆ **Adventure Wonderland, Christchurch (01202 483444).** Guaranteed fun whatever the weather for 2-12 year olds. Also Wild Thing indoor play centre with themed and interactive equipment, and Alice Maze.
www.adventurewonderland.co.uk

◆ **Beaulieu (01590 612345).** National Motor Museum – motoring heritage brought back to life. Includes James Bond Experience. Also 13th century Abbey and Monastic Life exhibition.
www.beaulieu.co.uk

◆ **Blue Reef Aquarium, Portsmouth (02392 875222).** Innovative displays provide an insight into the mysterious world of the deep. Restaurant and children's attractions.
www.bluereefaquarium.co.uk

◆ **Dinosaur Museum, Dorchester (01305 269741).** Children of all ages love these scaly creatures, so make for this superb "hands on" exhibition dedicated entirely to dinosaurs.
www.thedinosaurmuseum.com

◆ **Longdown Activity Farm, Ashurst, Near Southampton** (023 8029 2837). Lots of hands-on activities every day, including small animal handling sessions, plus indoor and outdoor play areas. Gift shop and tearoom.
www.longdownfarm.co.uk

◆ **Marwell Zoological Park, near Winchester (01962 777407).** 200-acre park with rare wild animals including tigers, zebras, cheetahs, leopards, etc. Children's zoo, picnic area, cafe.
www.marwell.org.uk

◆ **New Forest Museum and Visitor Centre, Lyndhurst (023 8028 3444).** Learn the story of the Forest in an audio-visual show; gift shop specialising in local crafts.
www.newforestmuseum.org.uk

◆ **Paultons Park, near Romsey (023 8081 4442).** A fun-filled day out at this family leisure park with rides and thrills galore. Over 40 attractions/rides.
www.paultonspark.co.uk

◆ **Tank Museum, Bovington, near Wareham (01929 405096).** Tanks and armoured cars from all over the world; "drive a tank" simulator; gift shop and restaurant.
www.tankmuseum.co.uk

◆ **Teddy Bear Museum, Dorchester (01305 266040).** From the earliest antique teddy bears to today's TV favourites, they are all waiting to greet you. Collectors' shop, House with family of human-size bears.
www.teddybearhouse.co.uk

Key to Symbols - see page 4
Please contact individual establishments to ensure that the facilities you require are available.

HAMPSHIRE & DORSET   **Board**

BOURNEMOUTH • Southbourne Grove Hotel   *Terms on request*

📨 12 🛏 12   ✕ BB   🐕   🍷   ⊘

CHARMOUTH • Cardsmill Farm Holidays   *B&B £26-£35pppn*

📨 4 🛏 4   BB   🛏 🪑   ⚠   ⊘

LULWORTH COVE • Cromwell House Hotel   *Terms on request*

📨 17 🛏 17   🍴 ✕   🛎 🛏 🪑 ◻   🐕 ♿ 🍷   🏃   Ⓐ

STUDLAND BAY • Knoll House Hotel   *Terms on request*

📨 80 🛏 56   🍴 ✕ BB 🛎 🛏 🪑 ◻ 🎠 ⚠ 🐕 ♿ 🍷 🏊 🏃 W   ⊘

HAMPSHIRE & DORSET   **Self-catering**

BOURNEMOUTH • Bournemouth Holiday Apartments   *£129-£998 per week*

🏨   🗄   🛏 🪑   🐕   ⊘

BRIDPORT • Lancombes House   *£350-£1900 per week*

🏠   🗐   🛏 🪑 🎠 ⚠ 🐕 ♿   W Ⓐ ⊘

CHARMOUTH • Cardsmill Farm Holidays   *Terms on request*

🏠   🎠 ⚠

DORCHESTER • Tamarisk Farm   *£260-£980 per week*

🏠   ⚠ 🐕   Ⓐ ⊘

LYME REGIS • Westover Farm Cottages   *Terms on request*

🏠   🗐   🛏 🪑 🎠   🐕

ROMSEY • Green Pastures Farm   *Terms on request*

                  🧺   ⚠ 🐕

For details of hundreds of properties throughout the UK visit:
www.holidayguides.com

ISLE OF WIGHT

⛏ Best Beaches ⛏

The varied coastline of the Isle of Wight includes many safe, sandy beaches. Colwell, Cowes, East Cowes, Gurnard, Seagrove, Springvale and Totland Bay have won a Quality Coast Award, and three beaches have earned the right to fly a Blue Flag.

BLUE FLAG BEACHES 2008

- *Sandown*
- *Shanklin*
- *Ventnor*

 Isle of Wight Tourism
- **Tel: 01983 813813**
- **Fax: 01983 823031**
- **e-mail: info@islandbreaks.co.uk**
- **www.islandbreaks.co.uk**

Ryde, Sea View & St Helens

 Family Fun Activities: Boating lake, bowling alley, swimming pool, ice skating rink, cinema • Dotto train along seafront and into town • Seaview Wildlife Encounter where children can hand-feed penguins, macaws and parrots • Travel back in time on the Isle of Wight steam railway.

☆ **Special Events: July:** Ryde Regatta. **August/September:** Ryde Carnival.

⛏ Beaches

- **BEACH.** Coastline three-and-a-half miles long; sand at Ryde, rockpools at Seaview; ample parking. *Safety and maintenance:* inshore rescue; cleaned daily. *Beach facilities:* canoe lake on esplanade, swimming pools, playground, mini fun fair, trampolines; snack bars and restaurants (some licensed); toilets with ♿ access. *Dog restrictions:* banned on main areas of beach from 1st May to 30th September; must be kept on lead on promenade; "poop scoop" regulations in force.

Sandown & Lake

Family Fun Activities: Fishing, tennis, basketball, putting, pitch and putt, crazy golf
- Pier with bowling and other attractions
- Street market • Zoo • Leisure centre
- Dinosaur Isle • Dotto train • Go-karts.

☆**Special Events:** July/August: Carnival. **August:** Regatta. **October:** White Air Extreme Sports Festival.

Beaches

• **BEACH.** Approximately three miles long, sandy with cliffs at back; promenade, pier complex with bar, restaurant, amusements and boat trips. *Safety and maintenance:* warning flags, lifeguards; cleaned daily in season. Kidzone in selected parts. *Beach facilities:* deck chairs, windsurfing, pedalcraft, children's entertainment; snack bars on promenade open during summer season; toilets with & access. *Dog restrictions:* banned from main areas of beach from 1st May to 30th September; "poop scoop"regulations in force.

Ventnor

Family Fun Activities: Botanic Gardens and Winter Gardens with regular entertainment • Golf • Paddling pool • Marina • Nearby Blackgang Chine has attractions and rides for the whole family.

☆ **Special Events:** **April:** Jazz Divas. **August:** Carnival.

Beaches

• **BEACH.** Approximately quarter-of-a-mile long; mainly sand, some shingle; promenade. *Safety and maintenance:* cleaned daily. *Beach facilities:* deck chairs; snack bars and restaurants, amusements; public house; toilets with & access. *Dog restrictions:* banned on main beach areas from 1st May to 30th September; "poop scoop" regulations in force.

Colwell & Totland

Small resort on Totland Bay, three miles south-west of Yarmouth.

Beaches

• **BEACH.** One-and-a-half miles long; sandy at Colwell, sand with some shingle at Totland; sea wall connects the two bays. *Safety and maintenance:* partly cleaned daily in season. *Beach facilities:* deck chairs and paddlecraft at Colwell; snacks and ice-cream at both locations. *Dog restrictions:* not allowed on Colwell beach between 1st May and 30th September.

Shanklin

Family Fun Activities: Water activities • Indoor play area, crazy golf, golf, putting • Dotto train • Cliff lift to town.

☆ **Special Events:** Shanklin Theatre shows. **August:** Shanklin Town regatta and sea events.

Beaches

• **BEACH.** Sandy beach, access via cliff lift; two-mile long promenade connects town to Sandown. Shanklin Chine illuminated on summer evenings. *Beach facilities:* refreshments, toilets; deck chairs, beach huts. *Dog restrictions:* banned from main beach from 1st May to 30th September.

Yarmouth

One of the oldest towns on the Island with a busy harbour. Boat trips to Needles from pier. Nearby attractions include Fort Victoria, Dimbola Lodge and Dinosaur Farm Museum.

☆ **Special Events:** **June:** Old Gaffers Festival.

Beaches

• **BEACH.** Shingle beach with pier; swimming at Sandhard area. *Beach facilities:* refreshments; toilets . *Dog restrictions:* must be kept on lead.

☆ Fun for all the Family ☆

◆ **Amazon World, Newchurch (01983 867122).** All-weather Amazon Rain Forest attraction with over 200 species of birds and animals. Falconry displays.
www.amazonworld.co.uk

◆ **Blackgang Chine, Chale (01983 730052).** 40 acres of cliff top gardens, exhibitions, fantasy attractions – Cowboy Town, Nurseryland, Giant Snakes 'n' Ladders, Water Force, a 100m high speed boat ride.
www.blackgangchine.com

◆ **Brickfields Horse Country, near Ryde (01983 566801).** From mighty Shires to miniature Shetland ponies. Unique collections of bygones, children's farm corner, restaurant and bar.
www.brickfields.net

◆ **Butterfly World and Fountain World, Wootton (01983 883430).** Hundreds of exotic butterflies and insects; displays of fountains and indoor gardens. Play area.

◆ **Dinosaur Isle, Sandown (01983 404344).** Exciting new exhibition centre in a spectacular pterosaur-shaped building, with life-size dinosaurs; guided fossil walks to sites of interest on the island.
www.dinosaurisle.com

◆ **Isle of Wight Steam Railway, Near Ryde (01983 882204).** 5½-mile round trip on genuine vintage train. Station at Havenstreet with museum, shop, cafe and bar.
www.iwsteamrailway.co.uk

◆ **Isle of Wight Wax Works, Brading (01983 407286/0870 4584477).** World-famous museum set in 11th century rectory mansion. Visit the Chamber of Horrors and Animal World.

◆ **Isle of Wight Zoo, Sandown (01983 405562).** Big cats, snakes and spiders. Cafe, play areas, animal contact area — be photographed with a snake!
www.isleofwightzoo.com

◆ **Natural History Centre, Godshill (01983 840333).** A fascinating display of tropical seashells, birds, butterflies and even a lizard embalmed in amber, all housed in a 17th century coach house.
www.shellmuseum.co.uk

◆ **Needles Park, Alum Bay (0870 458 0022).** A great family day out with attractions including chairlift, dare-devil rides, crazy golf, glass-making studio, sweet making; restaurant.
www.theneedles.co.uk

◆ **Osborne House, East Cowes (01983 200022).** Magnificent residence much loved by Queen Victoria. The 'Swiss Cottage' in the grounds was the playroom of the royal children; carriage rides through the grounds.

◆ **Robin Hill Country Park, near Newport (01983 527352).** Activities for all ages: Time Machine and Colossus rides; Countryside Centre, Play Village, Splash Attack and lots more.
www.robin-hill.com

◆ **Shipwreck Centre and Maritime Museum, Bembridge (01983 872223/ 873125).** Museum devoted to local maritime heritage. Shipwreck artefacts, ship models, diving equipment etc.

Key to Symbols - see page 4

Please contact individual establishments to ensure that the facilities you require are available.

ISLE OF WIGHT   Board

TOTLAND • Frenchman's Cove   *B&B £30-£50pppn*

🛏 10 🛁 10   BB   🛏 👶   Ⓐ ⊘

VENTNOR • Little Span Farm   *B&B £25-£27.50pppn*

🛏 4 🛁 4   BB   🛏 👶   🛝 🐕   Ⓐ ⊘

ISLE OF WIGHT   Self-catering

• Island Cottage Holidays   *Terms on request*

              🏠   📋   🛏 👶   🐕   Ⓐ

TOTLAND • The Coach House   *Terms on request*

🏨   📋 📑   🛏 👶   ⊘

VENTNOR • Ventnor Holiday Villas   *Terms on request*

🏨 🚐   🏠   📋   🛏 👶   🐕

VENTNOR • Little Span Farm   *£225-£725 per week*

              🏠   📋   👶 📻   🛝 🐕   Ⓐ ⊘

SUSSEX

 Best Beaches

Five beaches on this lively stretch of coast have earned 2008 Blue Flag awards after meeting a variety of strict criteria.

[i] South East England Tourism
• Tel: 023 8062 5400
• Fax: 023 8062 0010
• e-mail: enquiries@tourismse.com
• www.visitsoutheastengland.com

BLUE FLAG BEACHES 2008
• **West Wittering**
• **Eastbourne (Pier to Wish Tower)**
• **Littlehampton Coastguards**
• **Hove Lawns**
• **West Street**

For more information about holidaying in Sussex see:
• www.visitsussex.org
• www.sussexbythesea.com
• www.eastsussex.gov.uk

BRIGHTON

🏊 Family Fun Activities: Brighton Pier, Sea Life Centre, Royal Pavilion, Brighton Museum, British Engineerium, Preston Manor, Foredown Tower, West Blatchington Windmill, Fishing Museum, National Museum of Penny Slot Machines; Marina Village • Fishing, boat trips, windsurfing, sailing • Horse racing, greyhound racing • 10-pin bowling, putting, crazy golf, pitch and putt, golf courses, skate boarding, roller blading, ice skating, tennis, squash, bowls, badminton, cycle hire, indoor swimming pools • Cinemas, theatres, nightclubs, discos • Churchill Square, North Laine and Lanes shopping districts with family-friendly restaurants and cafes.

☆ Special Events: May: Brighton Festival. **June:** London-Brighton Bike Ride. **July:** Kite Festival. **August:** Circus. **November:** Veteran Car Run.

[i] **VisiitBrighton, Royal Pavilion Shop, 4-5 Pavilion Buildings, Brighton BNI IEE 0906 711 2255 brighton-tourism@brighton-hove.gov.uk www.visitbrighton.com**

🏖 Beaches

• **BEACH.** 7 miles long, shingle and rockpools; cliff walk, promenade with Volks Railway, pier with funfair and arcades. Artists' and fishing quarters. Naturist area at eastern end of promenade, near marina; warning flags, lifeguards (some undertow at extreme eastern end); cleaned daily in season. *Beach facilities:* deck chairs; ramp and lift to lower promenade; paddling pool, new children's play area; volleyball, basketball; showers; ice-cream kiosks, snack bars, restaurants and pubs; toilets with ♿ access, baby changing facilities. *Dog restrictions:* dogs allowed from West Pier to Hove boundary and from Volks Railway to Banjo Groyne. Not allowed on any other part of the beach.

BOGNOR REGIS

🏊 Family Fun Activities: Free summer Sunday afternoon bandstand concerts in Hotham Park • Playgrounds, amusement arcades, tennis, putting, crazy golf, golf course, sailing • Cinema • Day visitors welcome at Butlins Family Entertainment Centre • Miniature railway in Hotham Park.

☆ Special Events: Various events throughout the summer including: Bognor Birdman (the original), Sands of Time Seaside Festival, Illumination Gala and Procession, Here Comes Summer.

[i] **Visitor Information Centre, Belmont Street, Bognor Regis • 01243 823140 e-mail: bognorregis.vic@arun.gov.uk www.sussexbythesea.com**

🏖 Beaches

• **BEACH.** 8 miles long, sand and shingle, naturally sheltered; promenade and pier with arcades; ample voucher parking. *Safety and maintenance:* warning signs, rocks at low tide; cleaned regularly. *Beach facilities:* deck chairs, showers, children's play area; Kidcare Scheme along 50-metre stretch of seafront; seafront landtrain; ice-cream kiosks, snack bars, restaurants, pubs; toilets (toilets with ♿ access on sea front). *Dog restrictions:* not allowed on main beach from May to September.

EASTBOURNE

⛴ **Family Fun Activities:** Fort Fun and Treasure Island theme parks, Miniature Steam Railway, Sovereign Centre, Knockhatch Adventure Park, Drusillas Zoo, Seven Sisters Sheep Centre, Museum of Shops, Redoubt Fortress, Lifeboat Museum, historic Pevensey Castle and Michelham Priory, Victorian Pier with arcades, family pub and Camera Obscura • Multiplex cinema, four theatres, seafront bandstand, indoor karting, 10-pin bowling, tennis, mini-golf, Dotto Train, speedway stadium.

☆ **Special Events:** **May:** Magnificent Motors. **June:** Classic Motorcycle Run, International Tennis Championships **July:** Emergency Services Display. **August:** International Air Show, Family Festival of Tennis, Tennis championships; South of England Tennis championships. **September:** MG South Downs Run. **October:** Victorian Festival, Beer Festival.

ℹ Tourist Information Centre, Cornfield Road, Eastbourne BN21 4QA
0871 663 0031
e-mail: tic@eastbourne.gov.uk
www.visiteastbourne.com

🏖 Beaches

• **BEACH.** Five miles of beaches; shingle, sand and rockpools; promenade and pier with arcades, seafront cycleway; Dotto Train service; ample parking. *Safety and maintenance:* warning flags, lifeguards; Kidzone wristband scheme, first aid, rookie lifeguard classes. *Beach facilities:* deck chairs, sun loungers, parasols, beach huts, paddlecraft, water sports, boat trips, seafront bandstand, Punch & Judy; ice-cream kiosks, snack bars, restaurants and pubs; showers, toilets with ♿ access and baby changing facilities.

Sailing on
Eastbourne beach

☆ Fun for all the Family ☆

◆ **1066 Battle Abbey and Battlefield, Battle (01424 773792).** Founded by William the Conqueror to commemorate the Battle of Hastings in 1066. The battle site, Abbey ruins and grounds are open to the public.

◆ **Bentley Wildfowl and Motor Museum, near Lewes (01825 840573).** Hundreds of waterfowl and wildlife, including flamingos, cranes and peacocks, in 23 acres.
www.bentley.org.uk

◆ **Bluebell Railway, near Uckfield (01825 720800).** Collection of veteran locos from 1865 to 1958. Trains steam through miles of Sussex countryside.
www.bluebellrailway.co.uk

◆ **Buckley's Yesterday's World, Battle (01424 775378).** Experience a day in a bygone age and explore the re-created shop and room displays. Children's activity areas, gift shop, teas.
www.yesterdaysworld.co.uk

◆ **Drusillas Park, Alfriston (01323 874100).** Collection of rare cattle, exotic flamingos, waterfowl, monkeys and parrots. Farm playground, miniature railway, shops.
www.drusillas.co.uk

◆ **Earnley Butterflies & Gardens, Near Chichester (01243 512637).** Walk amongst amazing tropical butterflies, stroll through themed gardens, and explore life as it used to be in the Nostalgia Museum.
www.earnleybutterfliesandgardens.co.uk

◆ **Paradise Park, Newhaven (01273 512123).** Journey through time and see how plants and animals lived 200 million years ago. Miniature railway, gnome settlement.
www.paradisepark.co.uk

◆ **Royal Pavilion, Brighton (01273 290900).** The former seaside palace of George IV, with lavish Chinese-style interiors. Shop and tearoom.
www.royalpavilion.org.uk

◆ **Sea Life Centre Brighton (01273 604234).** Come face to face with thousands of fascinating sea creatures. Restaurants and shops.
www.sealife.co.uk

◆ **Seven Sisters Sheep Centre, Near Eastbourne (01323 423302).** Over 40 breeds of sheep - help feed the lambs in Spring, see the sheep being milked, or take a ride on the tractor trailer. We'll be pleased to meet 'ewe'!
www.sheepcentre.co.uk

◆ **A Smuggler's Adventure, Hastings (01424 444412).** Relive the dangers and excitement that faced smugglers and customs men in times past. Displays and tableaux with life-sized figures .
www.smugglersadventure.co.uk

◆ **Weald and Downland Open Air Museum, near Chichester (01243 811363).** A collection of historic buildings, 16th century treadwheel etc saved from destruction. Heavy horses, shop, cafe.
www.wealddown.co.uk

Key to Symbols - see page 4

Please contact individual establishments to ensure that the facilities you require are available.

SUSSEX   Board

HASTINGS • Grand Hotel   *Terms on request*

🛏 14 👤 14   ✕ BB   ♀   W Ⓐ ⊘

SUSSEX   Self-catering

BATTLE • Crowhurst Park   *Terms on request*

🏠   ⬛   🐎 ⚠   ♀ ⌇   W

CHIDDINGLY • Pekes Manor   *Terms on request*

🏠   ⚠ 🐕   ⌇

HENFIELD • New Hall Holiday Flat & Cottage   *Terms on request*

KENT

 Best Beaches

A record number of beaches on the Kent coast have gained the prestigious Blue Flag Award for the highest standards of beach management and cleanliness.

BLUE FLAG BEACHES 2008

- *Herne Bay*
- *Birchington Minnis Bay*
- *Margate Main Sands*
- *Margate Westbrook Bay*
- *Margate Walpole Bay*
- *St Mildreds Bay, Westgate*
- *West Bay Westgate*
- *Botany Bay, Westgate*
- *Stone Bay, Broadstairs*
- *Tankerton*
- *Ramsgate Main Sands*
- *Joss Bay*

[i] **South East England Tourism**
- **Tel: 023 8062 5400**
- **Fax: 023 8062 0010**
- **e-mail: enquiries@tourismse.com**
- **www.visitsoutheastengland.com**

For more information about holidaying in Kent see:
- www.visitkent.co.uk
- www.heartofkent.org.uk
- www.kentattractions.co.uk

BROADSTAIRS

🎪 **Family Fun Activities:** Ice-cream parlours, amusement arcade, Pavilion with all-year entertainment, bandstand • Tennis, putting, golf course, crazy golf, bowls, angling, sailing • Award-winning St Peter's Village Tour • Skate park and climbing centre • Dickens House, Crampton Tower Museum.

☆ **Special Events: June:** Dickens Festival Week. **July:** Sea Sunday. **August:** Water Gala Day. Folk Week **September:** Open Bowls Tournament.

ℹ️ **Visitor Information Centre, (in Dickens House Museum), 2 Victoria Parade, Broadstairs CT10 1QS**
0870 264 6111
e-mail: tourism@thanet.gov.uk
www.visitthanet.co.uk

⛱️ Beaches

• **VIKING BAY.** Sandy beach, 150 metres long; promenade, harbour, pier and boardwalk, parking; ♿ access. *Safety and maintenance:* first-aid station, warning flags, animal logo signposts; lifeguards, bay inspector/information; cleaned daily. *Beach facilities:* deck chairs/sun loungers and chalets for hire, children's rides, donkey rides, Punch and Judy (August only); pubs, cafes, shops and restaurants nearby, amusements, surfski/belly boards; lift to beach; toilets (toilets with ♿ RADAR key access Albion Road car park, Broadstairs Harbour, and Victoria Gardens). *Dog restrictions:* not permitted on beach 1 May to 30 September incl.

• **STONE BAY.** 200 metres long, sandy with chalk cliffs and rockpools; promenade; ♿ access. *Safety and maintenance:* cleaned daily; lifeguards. *Beach facilities:* chalets for hire. Cafes and restaurants nearby. Toilets. *Dog restrictions:* banned 15 May to 15 September between 10am and 6pm.

• **LOUISA BAY.** 150 metres long, quiet sandy bay; promenade. Disabled access via fairly steep slope. *Safety and maintenance:* warning signs; beach cleaned daily. *Beach facilities:* chalets for hire; cafe, tidal pool. *Dog restrictions:* "poop scoop" beach.

• **JOSS BAY.** 200 metres long, sandy beach, parking, ♿ access. *Safety and maintenance:* warning flags, lifeguards; cleaned daily; animal logo signposts to help children find their way back to parents. *Beach facilities:* deck chairs for hire, surf skis/belly boards; lessons; cafe; toilets with ♿ RADAR key access Easter-Sep. *Dog restrictions:* not permitted 10am-6pm 15 May-15 Sept; "poop scoop" beach.

• **KINGSGATE BAY.** 150 metres long; quiet and secluded sandy beach. *Safety and maintenance:* cleaned daily. *Beach facilities:* chalets for hire; clifftop pub. *Dog restrictions:* "poop scoop" beach.

• **BOTANY BAY.** 200 metres long, sandy beach; ♿ access. *Safety and maintenance:* lifeguards/bay inspector; warnings, cleaned daily. *Beach facilities:* cafe, clifftop pub; toilets. *Dog restrictions:* not permitted 10am-6pm 15 May-15 Sept.

• **DUMPTON GAP.** Quiet sandy bay with some rocks, 150 metres long; promenade and parking. Disabled access. *Safety and maintenance:* warning signs; cleaned daily. *Beach facilities:* chalets for hire; cafe; toilets. *Dog restrictions:* "poop scoop" beach.

MARGATE

🎪 **Family Fun Activities:** Heated indoor leisure pool, indoor sports/leisure centre, amusement arcades • Shell Grotto, The Droit House, Margate Museum (contact VIC before visiting) •Lifeboat Station • Ten-pin bowling, bowls, indoor bowls, tennis, putting, pitch and putt, golf course, mini-golf, crazy golf, adventure golf, angling • Casino, theatres, nightclubs, disco, bandstand.

☆ **Special Events: Feb/March:** Quad Bike Racing. **June:** Great Bucket & Spade Run, Margate Big Event. **June/July:** Open Bowls Tournament, Volleyball Competition. **July:** Big Sky Jazz Festival. **August:** Carnival Parade. **September:** Kite Festival.

[i] **Visitor Information Centre, 12-13 The Parade, Margate CT9 1EY**
0870 264 6111
e-mail: tourism@thanet.gov.uk
www.visitthanet.co.uk

Beaches

• **MARGATE MAIN SANDS.** rejuvenated harbour area with cafes/bars; 200 metres long, sandy beach, promenade and boardwalk, parking, & access. *Safety and maintenance:* warning flags, animal logo signposts to help children find their way back to parents, first-aid station, lifeguards and lifeboat; bay inspector/ information, beach cleaned daily. *Beach facilities:* sun loungers, deckchairs for hire; tidal boating pool, paddlecraft, donkey rides; kiddies' corner; cafes, restaurants, pubs; toilets with & access. *Dog restrictions:* not permitted on beach 1 May to 30 September incl.

• **PALM BAY/HODGES GAP & FORENESS POINT.** 200 metres long; sandy, sheltered beach, parking. *Safety and maintenance:* cleaned daily. *Beach facilities:* designated water-ski and jet ski area; toilets. *Dog restrictions:* "poop scoop" beach.

• **WALPOLE BAY.** Sandy beach 400 metres long, popular watersports bay, tidal pool, lift, promenade, parking, & access. *Safety and maintenance:* warning flags, lifeguards; cleaned daily. *Beach facilities:* chalets and jet skis for hire; cafe, toilets. Monthly Farmers' Market. *Dog restrictions:* dog ban 1 May to 30 September incl.

• **WESTBROOK BAY.** 200 metres long, sandy; promenade and parking. *Safety and maintenance:* warning flags, lifeguards, bay inspector/information; first-aid station; cleaned daily. *Beach facilities:* deck chairs,

chalets for hire; designated water ski area; adventure golf; cafe; toilets with & access. *Dog restrictions:* banned from 15 May to 15 September 10am to 6pm.

RAMSGATE

🏊 **Family Fun Activities:** Heated indoor leisure pool, sports and leisure centre • Maritime Museum (contact VIC before visiting) • Royal harbour and yacht marina • Amusement arcades, leisure park and boating pool, tennis, bowls, angling • Theatre, cinema, discos.

☆ **Special Events: July:** Powerboat and Waterski Grand Prix, Carnival Parade, Costumed Walks. **August:** Open Bowls Tournament, International Sailing Week. **September:** Model Ships Rally.

[i] **Visitor Information Centre, 17 Albert Court, York Street, Ramsgate CT11 9DN • 0870 264 6111**
e-mail: tourism@thanet.gov.uk
www.visitthanet.co.uk

Beaches

• **MAIN SANDS.** Popular sandy beach, 250 metres long; promenade and parking, & access. *Safety and maintenance:* animal logo signposts to help children find their way back to their parents, warning flags, lifeguards, bay inspector/information; first-aid station; beach cleaned daily. *Beach facilities:* donkey rides; deck chairs, sun loungers for hire; amusements, children's play area; cafes, restaurants, pubs, shops; toilets with & access; Edwardian lift to beach. *Dog restrictions:* not permitted on beach 1 May to 30 September incl.

• **PEGWELL BAY.** A stretch of unprotected sea cliffs with great geological interest. Part of Kent's largest national Nature Reserve. Toilets, cafe, picnic area, parking.

☆ Fun for all the Family ☆

◆ **A Day at the Wells, Royal Tunbridge Wells (01892 546545).** Experience the sights and sounds of 18th century Tunbridge Wells. Special commentary for children.

◆ **Canterbury Tales, Canterbury (01227 479227).** Chaucer's 14th century tales brought vividly to life by the latest audio-visual technology.
www.canterburytales.org.uk

◆ **Eagle Heights, Eynsford (01322 866577).** One of the UK's largest bird of prey centres with over 50 species of raptors. Daily flying demonstrations, and collection of reptiles and mammals.
www.eagleheights.co.uk

◆ **Finchcocks, Goudhurst (01580 211702).** Living museum of early keyboard instruments, played whenever the house is open.
www.finchcocks.co.uk

◆ **Historic Dockyard, Chatham (01634 823800).** Step back 200 years at the world's most complete Georgian dockyard, now a living museum. New permanent lifeboat exhibition.
www.chdt.org.uk

◆ **The Hop Farm at the Kentish Oast Village, Paddock Wood (0870 0274166).** Exhibitions and displays of hop picking and shop life in Victorian times. Indoor and outdoor play areas, animal farm and pets' corner.
www.thehopfarm.co.uk

◆ **Howletts Wild Animal Park, near Canterbury (01303 264647).** Caged and free-roaming animals including tigers and gorillas. Teas, picnics.
www.howletts.net

◆ **Kent and East Sussex Steam Railway** operates 80-minute steam train rides from Tenterden Town Station to Northiam (**01580 765155**).
www.kesr.org.uk

◆ **Museum of Kent Life, Cobtree (01622 763936).** History of the county in displays and live exhibits. Rare breeds and farm animals; play area.
www.museum-kentlife.co.uk

◆ **Romney, Hythe and Dymchurch Railway (01797 362353).** Runs from Hythe to Dungeness – 80 minute journey through beautiful landscape.
www.rhdr.org.uk

◆ **South of England Rare Breeds Centre, Ashford (01233 861493).** Set in 120 acres of unspoilt countryside - friendly farm animals, indoor and outdoor play areas, Discovery Garden.
www.rarebreeds.org.uk

◆ **Wingham Bird Park, near Canterbury (01227 720836).** Set in 25 acres of beautiful countryside, with large walk-through aviaries, reptile house, adventure playground.

Reach Court Farm Cottages, St Margaret's Bay

Situated in the heart of a family-run, working farm, surrounded by open countryside, these five luxury self-contained cottages are very special. They are set around the old farm yard in an attractive setting of lawns and shrubs with open views from the front or rear. The cottages sleep from two to six plus cot, and the accommodation is of the highest standard, giving them a relaxing country feel, with the kitchens equipped with ovens, fridges, microwaves, toasters, coffee makers, etc. There is also a washing machine and tumble dryer in an adjoining laundry room.

Reach Court Farm is the nearest farm to France and was known as the "Front Line Farm" during World War II. St Margaret's is a rural village with shops and public houses offering a range of eating facilities. Dover, Folkestone, Canterbury and Sandwich are all within easy reach.

Mrs J. Mitchell, Reach Court Farm, St Margaret's-at-Cliff, St Margaret's Bay, Dover CT15 6AQ Tel & Fax: 01304 852159

e-mail: enquiries@reachcourtfarmcottages.co.uk • www.reachcourtfarmcottages.co.uk

Key to Symbols - see page 4

Please contact individual establishments to ensure that the facilities you require are available.

KENT

Board

ASHFORD • Bolden's Wood			B&B £25pppn
🛏 2	BB 🍽	🅰	Ⓐ 🚭

CANTERBURY • South Wootton House		Terms on request
🛏 1 🛁 1	BB	Ⓐ 🚭

CANTERBURY • Upper Ansdore		Terms on request
🛏 5 🛁 5	BB	🐕 🚭

DOVER • Maison Dieu Guest House			B&B £23.50-£27.50pppn
🛏 7 🛁 5	BB 🛏 🕯		W Ⓐ 🚭

KENT

Self-catering

ST MARGARET'S BAY • Reach Court Farm Cottages			Terms on request
🏠	📘	🅰	🎣

LONDON & HOME COUNTIES

ℹ Visit London
1 Warwick Row, London SW1E 5ER
• **Tel: 020 7932 2000**
• **Fax: 020 7932 0222**
e-mail: enquiries@visitlondon.com
• **www.visitlondon.com**
  www.kidslovelondon.com

HISTORIC BUILDINGS

◆ **Hampton Court, East Molesey, Surrey (020 8781 9500).** Built over 400 years ago, this became one of Henry VIII's royal palaces. Tudor tennis court, Great Vine and Maze. Nearest BR station: Hampton Court.

◆ **Houses of Parliament and Strangers' Gallery**: if you wish to listen to a debate apply in advance to your MP or join the queue at St Stephen's Entrance on the day.

◆ **Kensington Palace (0870 751 5170).** State Apartments of the late Stuart and Hanoverian periods containing 17th century furniture and pictures. Nearest Tube: Queensway.

◆ **St Paul's Cathedral (020 7246 8348).** Sir Christopher Wren's masterpiece built between 1675 and 1710. Nearest Tube: St Paul's, Mansion House.

◆ **Tower of London (020 7709 0765).** Built by William the Conqueror as a fortress, this magnificent building today houses the Crown Jewels. Nearest Tube: Tower Hill.

◆ **Westminster Abbey (020 7222 7110).** Founded by Edward the Confessor in 1065, the Abbey has become the burial place of many famous people. Nearest Tube: Westminster.

MUSEUMS & GALLERIES

British Museum (020 7323 8000).
Imperial War Museum (020 7416 5000).
Museum of London (020 7600 3699).
National Gallery (020 7839 3321).
National Maritime Museum (020 8858 4422).
National Portrait Gallery (020 7312 2463).
Natural History Museum (020 7942 5000).
Royal Academy of Arts (020 7300 8000).
Science Museum (020 7938 8000).
Tate Britain (020 7887 8008).
Tate Modern (020 7887 8734).
Victoria & Albert Museum (020 7942 2197).

◆ **Bethnal Green Museum of Childhood (020 8983 5200).** A child's world of toys, dolls, dolls' houses, children's costumes.
www.museumofchildhood.org.uk

◆ **London Transport Museum (020 7379 6344)**. A collection of historic vehicles illustrating the development of London's transport system. Nearest Tube: Covent Garden.
www.ltmuseum.co.uk

VISITOR ATTRACTIONS

◆ **British Airways London Eye, South Bank, London (0870 5000 600)**. Stunning views over Central London and beyond during a half-hour ride on the gently moving 135m high observational wheel.
www.londoneye.com

◆ **Chessington World of Adventures (0870 444 7777)**. Exciting theme areas, rides, circus and zoo – a world of adventure for all the family. BR: Chessington South.
www.chessington.com

◆ **HMS Belfast (020 7940 6328)**. The last survivor of the Royal Navy's big ships, now a permanent floating museum. Nearest Tube: London Bridge.
www.iwm.org.uk/belfast

◆ **Kew Gardens, near Richmond (020 8332 5655)**. 300 acres, once belonging to the Royal family, now contains 25000 different plant species; greenhouses, herbarium and museums. Tube: Kew Gardens.
www.rbgkew.org.uk

◆ **Legoland, Windsor (08705 040404)**. A theme park with a difference, all set in 150 acres of wooded parkland.
www.lego.com

◆ **London Dungeon (020 7403 7221)**. The world's first medieval horror exhibition featuring gruesome scenes of torture, murder and depravation. Perfect for the kids! Nearest Tube: London Bridge.
www.dungeons.co.uk

◆ **London Zoo (020 7722 3333)**. One of the largest zoos in the world containing a varied collection of animals, birds, reptiles and insects. New Children's Zoo tells how people and animals live side by side. Nearest Tube: Camden Town.
www.londonzoo.co.uk

◆ **Madame Tussaud's (0870 400 3000)**. The world famous waxworks of contemporary and historic figures complete with the inevitable Chamber of Horrors. Nearest Tube: Baker Street.
www.madame-tussauds.com

◆ **Royal Observatory, Greenwich (020 8858 4422)**. Includes Wren's Flamsteed House, Meridian Building and Planetarium. New high precision pendulum clock donated by Moscow Research Centre.
www.nmm.ac.uk

The Tower of London

The Athena

110-114 SUSSEX GARDENS, HYDE PARK, LONDON W2 1UA
Tel: 0207 706 3866; Fax: 0207 262 6143
E-Mail: athena@stavrouhotels.co.uk www.stavrouhotels.co.uk

TREAT YOURSELVES TO A QUALITY HOTEL AT AFFORDABLE PRICES

The Athena is a newly completed family run hotel in a restored Victorian building. Professionally designed, including a lift to all floors and exquisitely decorated, we offer our clientele the ambience and warm hospitality necessary for a relaxing and enjoyable stay. Ideally located in a beautiful tree-lined avenue, extremely well-positioned for sightseeing London's famous sights and shops; Hyde Park, Madame Tussaud's, Oxford Street, Marble Arch, Knightsbridge, Buckingham Palace and many more are all within walking distance.

Travel connections to all over London are excellent, with Paddington and Lancaster Gate Stations, Heathrow Express, A2 Airbus and buses minutes away.
Our tastefully decorated bedrooms have en suite bath/shower rooms, satellite colour TV, bedside telephones, tea/coffee making facilities. Hairdryers, trouser press, laundry and ironing facilities available on request. Car parking available.

Stavrou Hotels is a family-run group of hotels.
We offer quality and convenience at affordable rates.
A VERY WARM WELCOME AWAITS YOU.

Single Rooms from £50-£89
Double/Twin Rooms from £64-£99
Triple & Family Rooms from £25 per person
All prices include full English breakfast plus VAT.

Our hotels accept all major Credit cards, but some charges may apply.

Stavrou Hotels

Gower Hotel

129 SUSSEX GARDENS,
HYDE PARK, LONDON W2 2RX

Tel: 0207 262 2262
Fax: 0207 262 2006

e-mail: gower@stavrouhotels.co.uk
www.stavrouhotels.co.uk

The Gower Hotel is a small family-run Hotel, centrally located, within two minutes' walk from Paddington Station, which benefits from the Heathrow Express train "15 minutes to and from Heathrow Airport". Excellently located for sightseeing London's famous sights and shops, Hyde Park, Madame Tussaud's, Oxford Street, Harrods, Marble Arch, Buckingham Palace and many more close by. All rooms have private shower and WC, radio, TV (includes satellite and video channels), direct dial telephone and tea and coffee facilities. All recently refurbished and fully centrally heated. 24 hour reception.

All prices are inclusive of a large traditional English Breakfast & VAT

Single Rooms from £30-£79 • Double/Twin Rooms from £60-£89 • Triple & Family Rooms from £80
• Discount available on 3 nights or more if you mention this advert

Queens Hotel

33 Anson Road, Tufnell Park,
LONDON N7 0RB
Tel: 0207 607 4725
Fax: 0207 697 9725

e-mail: queens@stavrouhotels.co.uk
www.stavrouhotels.co.uk

The Queens Hotel is a large double-fronted Victorian building standing in its own grounds five minutes' walk from Tufnell Park Station. Quietly situated with ample car parking spaces; 15 minutes to West End and close to London Zoo, Hampstead and Highgate. Two miles from Kings Cross and St Pancras Stations. Many rooms en suite. **All prices include full English Breakfast plus VAT. Children at reduced prices. Discounts on longer stays.**

Single Rooms from £30-£55 • Double/Twin Rooms from £40-£69 • Triple & Family Rooms from £20 per person

Stavrou Hotels is a family-run group of hotels.

We offer quality and convenience at affordable rates.

A VERY WARM WELCOME AWAITS YOU

Our hotels accept all major Credit cards, but some charges may apply.

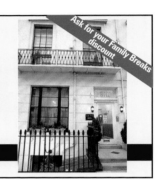
Key to Symbols - see page 4
Please contact individual establishments to ensure that the facilities you require are available.

LONDON & HOME COUNTIES

Board

KINGSTON-UPON-THAMES • Chase Lodge Hotel *Terms on request*

🛏 11 🛁 11   ♿ ✕ BB 🍽 🎱 ♿   🐕   ♀   Ⓐ

LONDON • The Athena *Terms on request*

BB   Ⓐ

LONDON • Barry House *Terms on request*

🛏 18 🛁 15   BB

LONDON • Gower Hotel *Terms on request*

🛏 21 🛁 19   BB   Ⓐ

LONDON • Queens Hotel *Terms on request*

BB   Ⓐ

EAST OF ENGLAND

Best Beaches

A very impressive total of 12 beaches in this area were proud winners in 2008 of the European Blue Flag for beaches meeting the strictest of standards. Several beaches also were proud winners of a Quality Coast Award.

[i] **East of England Tourism**
Bedfordshire, Cambridgeshire, Essex, Hertfordshire, Norfolk, Suffolk).

- Tel: **01284 727470**
- Fax: **01284 706657**
- e-mail: **info@eet.ork.uk**
- **www.visiteastofengland.com**

BLUE FLAG BEACHES 2008
- *Dovercourt Bay*
- *Southend*
  Shoebury Common
  Shoeburyness
  Jubilee
- *Cromer*
- *Mundesley*
- *Sea Palling*
- *Lowestoft*
  North
  South of Pier
- *Southwold Pier*
- *Felixstowe South*
- *Brightlingsea*

For more information about holidaying in East Anglia see:
- *www.visitbeds-luton.com* • *www.midbeds.gov.uk* • *www.bedford.gov.uk*
- *wwww.vistcambridge.org*
- *www.essex-sunshine-coast.org.uk* • *www.realessex.co.uk*
- *www.hertfordshire.com*
- *wwww.visitnorfolk.co.uk www.northnorfolk.org*
- *wwww.visit-suffolk.org.uk* • *www.visitsuffolkattractions.co.uk*

CLACTON-ON-SEA

Family Fun Activities: Fun-packed pier with rides, amusements, cafes and fishing (wheelchair accessible) • Leisure centre with swimming pool • Two theatres, cinema, bingo, night clubs • Clacton Factory Shopping Village.

[i] Tourist Information Centre, Town Hall, Station Road, Clacton-on-Sea CO15 1SE • 01255 686633
e-mail: clactontic@tendringdc.gov.uk
www.essex-sunshine-coast.org.uk

Beaches

• BEACH. Long sandy beach, gently sloping. *Beach facilities:* deck chairs, beach cafes; toilets. *Dog restrictions:* dogs banned on some beaches during main holiday season.

SOUTHEND

Family Fun Activities: Pier (longest pleasure pier in the world), Sea Life Adventure, Cliffs Pavilion, Adventure Island • Sailing, water ski-ing, windsurfing, motor boats, marine activity centre • Indoor swimming pools, skateboard park, tennis, bowls, golf, miniature golf, putting, children's playgrounds • Museums, planetarium, art gallery; theatres, nightclubs, discos • The Kursaal indoor entertainments centre

[i] Visitor Information Centre, Southend Pier, Western Esplanade, Southend-on-Sea SS1 1EE
01702 215120 • Fax: 01702 431449
www.visitsouthend.co.uk

Beaches

• BEACHES. 7 miles of sea and foreshore with sand and shingle beach, stretching from Shoeburyness to Chalkwell and Leigh; ample parking. *Safety and maintenance:* cleaned daily boards with information on bathing water quality. *Beach facilities:* paddling pool, activity frame, beach shower; cafes, restaurants; toilets. *Dog restrictions:* from 1st May to 30th September must be kept on a lead on promenade.

GREAT YARMOUTH

Family Fun Activities: Yesterday's World, Marina Leisure Centre, Hollywood Indoor Golf, Pleasure Beach, Sea Life Centre, House of Wax, Model Village, Joyland Fun Park, "Amazonia" The Jungle at the Winter gardens - children's adventure play.• Stock car racing, greyhound racing, horse racing, golf; putting, pitch and putt, outdoor bowls, ten-pin bowling, indoor karting • Marina, boating, fishing, sea cruises, Broads cruises, horse riding, indoor swimming pools, squash, tennis amusement arcades, children's playgrounds, Pirates' Cove (novelty golf), piers, road train • Museums, theatres, circus, cinema, nightclubs.

☆ **Special Events:** Fireworks Displays, Herring Festival, Festival of Bowls, Maritime Festival. Carnivals and fêtes, band concerts.

[i] Tourist Information Centre, 25 Marine Parade, Great Yarmouth NR30 2EN • 01493 846346
e-mail: tourism@great-yarmouth.gov.uk
www.great-yarmouth.co.uk

🏖 Beaches.

• **GREAT YARMOUTH BEACH.** Sandy beach, five miles long; two piers with entertainment. *Safety and maintenance:* warning flags, lifeguards; cleaned regularly. *Beach facilities:* deck chairs, windbreaks, beach huts; trampolines, donkey rides, inflatables, horse drawn landaus, pleasure boat trips; ice-cream kiosks, snack bars, restaurants and pubs; toilets on sea front with ♿ access. *Dog restrictions:* banned from beach during main season.

• **GORLESTON BEACH.** One and a half miles long, sandy; promenade and pier with good parking adjacent. *Safety and maintenance:* warning flags, lifeguards; beach cleaned during summer season. *Beach facilities:* deck chairs, trampolines, beach huts and chalets; ice-cream kiosks, snack bars, restaurants and pubs; toilets with ♿ access. *Dog restrictions:* banned from Blue Flag section during main summer months.

LOWESTOFT

🏠 Family Fun Activities: Mayhem soft play area, museums, pier; swimming pool, indoor football centre, adventure golf, golf, putting, pitch and putt, tennis, bowling, horse riding, water sports, parks with children's playgrounds • Theatres, cinemas, discos, nightclubs. Nearby: New Pleasurewood Hills, Suffolk Wildlife Park, Transport Museum, Lowestoft Ness (Britain's most easterly point).

ⓘ **Tourist Information Centre, East Point Pavilion, Royal Plain, Lowestoft NR33 0AP • 01502 533600 e-mail: touristinfo@waveney.gov.uk www.visit-lowestoft.co.uk Brochure info line: 0870 6061303**

🏖 Beaches

• **KESSINGLAND BEACH.** Pebble and shingle with some sand; low cliffs, easy access. *Safety and maintenance:* cleaned by Local Authority. *Dog restrictions:* banned from 1st May to 30th September; must be kept on lead on promenade.

• **PAKEFIELD BEACH.** Sandy beach with some shingle below low grassy cliffs; parking. *Safety and maintenance:* cleaned by Local Authority; dangerous to clamber or swim near groynes. *Beach facilities:* pubs; toilets with ♿ access.

• **LOWESTOFT RESORT BEACHES.** Sandy pleasure beaches with two piers; esplanade and ample parking. *Safety and maintenance:* warning flags, lifeguards; dangerous to clamber or swim near groynes; cleaned daily. *Beach facilities:* children's corner, chalets, ice-cream kiosks, restaurants, snack bars, pubs; toilets with ♿ access. *Dog restrictions:* banned from 1st May to 30th September; must be kept on lead on promenade.

• **SOUTHWOLD RESORT BEACH.** Part sand, part shingle with sand dunes; refurbished pier including amusements and refreshments. Parking. *Safety and maintenance:* warning flags, lifeguards; cleaned by Local Authority. *Beach facilities:* beach huts; cafes, pubs; toilets. *Dog restrictions:* banned from 1st May to 30th September; must be kept on lead on promenade.

• **SOUTHWOLD DENES.** Part sand, part shingle with sand dunes. This rural beach is secluded and peaceful, an ideal place for walkers and nature enthusiasts. Parking. *Safety and maintenance:* cleaned by Local Authority.

☆ Fun for all the Family ☆

BEDFORDSHIRE

◆ **Whipsnade Wild Animal Park, Dunstable (01582 872171).** Britain's largest conservation centre specialising in breeding certain endangered species. Children's zoo, steam railway.
www.whipsnade.co.uk

◆ **Woburn Safari Park (01525 290407).** Britain's largest drive-through safari park. Roundabouts and rides.
www.woburnsafari.co.uk

CAMBRIDGESHIRE

◆ **Nene Valley Railway, Peterborough (01780 784444).** A preserved steam railway with 7½ miles of track. Cafe shop, museum and engine shed.
www.nvr.org.uk

◆ **Sacrewell Farm and Country Centre, Thornaugh (01780 782254).** 500-acre farm with working watermill, nature trails, displays of farming bygones.
www.sacrewell.org.uk

ESSEX

◆ **Colchester Zoo, Colchester (01206 331292).** World-wide collection of animals and birds, with daily displays of parrots, sealions and falcons. Penguin parade, snake handling, meet the elephants.
www.colchester-zoo.co.uk

HERTFORDSHIRE

◆ **Paradise Wildlife Park, Broxbourne (01992 470490).** 17 acres with lots of animals; woodland railway, pony rides, aviary, education centre.
www.pwpark.com

NORFOLK

◆ **Banham Zoo, Banham (01953 887771).** Over 25 acres of wildlife in parkland setting with extensive collection of rare and endangered species. Road train, adventure playground and World of Penguins.
www.banhamzoo.co.uk

◆ **Dinosaur Adventure Park, Weston Longville (01603 876310).** Walk through woodland to view dinosaurs in natural settings. Adventure rides, play area, wooded maze; bygones museum.
www.dinosaurpark.co.uk

◆ **Sea Life Centre, Great Yarmouth (01493 330631).** A spectacular way to experience the underwater world, with themed tanks on local marine life.
www.sealife.co.uk

SUFFOLK

◆ **Easton Farm Park, Wickham Market (01728 746475).** Victorian farm setting for many species of farm animals including rare breeds. Nature trail, pets paddock and adventure playground.

◆ **Pleasurewood Hills Family Theme Park, Lowestoft (01502 586000).** Live shows and all the rides your family can handle! Off A12 between Great Yarmouth and Lowestoft.
www.pleasurewoodhills.co.uk

◆ **Suffolk Wildlife Park, Kessingland (01502 740291).** Suffolk's "walking safari" set in 100 acres of dramatic coastal parkland. Daily feeding sessions, safari road train, adventure playground.
www.suffolkwildlifepark.co.uk

EAST OF ENGLAND
Board

AYLSHAM • Old Pump House — *Terms on request*

🛏 5 🛁 5   ✕ BB   🐴   W   ⊘

FRAMLINGHAM • High House Farm — *Terms on request*

🛏 2 🛁 2   BB   🛏 ♿   ⚊

EAST OF ENGLAND
Self-catering

BACTON-ON-SEA • Castaways Holiday Park — *Terms on request*

🏠   🏡   🧺   ⚊ 🐴   🍷   Ⓐ

KESSINGLAND • Kessingland Cottage — *£95-£375 per week*

🏠   🐴 ♿   ⊘

LOWESTOFT • Beach Farm Residential & Holiday Park — *Terms on request*

🚐 🏡   ⚊ 🐴   🍷   ⸚

NAYLAND • Gladwins Farm — *Terms on request*

🏡 🏠   🛏 ♿   🐴   W

SOUTHWOLD • Durrants & H.A. Adnams Holiday Letting — *Terms on request*

🏠   🐴   Ⓐ ⊘

SUDBURY • Plough House — *Terms on request*

🏠   🐴

WINTERTON-ON-SEA • The Timbers — *Terms on request*

🏠   🗐   🛏   🐴

MIDLANDS

Best Beaches

Three beaches in the East Midlands area have attained the standards necessary to have won a Blue Flag for 2008.

BLUE FLAG BEACHES 2008
- *Mablethorpe*
- *Skegness*
- *Sutton on Sea*

[i] **East Midlands Tourism**
(Leicestershire & Rutland, Lincolnshire, Northamptonshire, Nottinghamshire, Peak District & Derbyshire).

www.enjoyenglandseastmidlands.com

For other counties in the Midlands see individual Tourist Boards (below)

For more information about holidaying in the Midlands see:
- www.glos-cotswolds.com
- www.visitherefordshire.co.uk
- www.shropshiretourism.info
- www.enjoystaffordshire.com
- www.visitnorthernwarwickshire.com
- www.visitshakespeare-country.co.uk
- www.worcestershire-tourism.org

☆ Fun for all the Family ☆

DERBYSHIRE

◆ **Gulliver's Kingdom, Matlock Bath. (01925 444888).** Theme park set in 15 acres of wooded hillside, designed especially for younger children.
www.gulliversfun.co.uk

◆ **Heights of Abraham, Matlock Bath. (01629 582365).** Spectacular cable car ride to hilltop country park. Show caverns, visitor centre, restaurant.
www.heights-of-abraham.co.uk

◆ **National Tramway Museum, Crich. (01773 854321).** Tramcars from all over the world; scenic displays, restaurant, children's playground.
www.tramway.co.uk

GLOUCESTERSHIRE

◆ **National Waterways Museum, Gloucester. (01452 318200).** Recreates the story of Britain's inland waterways. Working machinery, demonstrations.
www.nwm.org.uk

◆ **Slimbridge Wildfowl and Wetlands Centre, Slimbridge (01453 891900).** Over 2300 birds of 180 different species, including in winter wild swans, geese and ducks. Activities throughout the year.
www.wwt.org.uk

◆ **Sudeley Castle, Winchcombe. (01242 602308).** Toys, treasures, peacock gardens, children's play area. Katherine Parr (Henry VIII's Queen) buried here.
www.sudeleycastle.co.uk

LEICESTERSHIRE

◆ **Moira Furnace & Craft Workshops, Near Ashby de la Zouch. (01283 224667).** Impressive l9th century blast furnace museum. Woodland walks, nature trail, children's play area.

◆ **Snibston Discovery Park, Coalville. (01530 278444).** Exhibition hall with 5 galleries exploring the county's industrial heritage, plus outdoor science play area, colliery tours.

LINCOLNSHIRE

◆ **Natureland Seal Sanctuary, Skegness (01754 764345).** Entertainment, education and conservation: baby seals, penguins, free-flight tropical birds, plus lots of other fascinating creatures.
www.skegnessnatureland.co.uk

◆ **National Fishing Heritage Centre, Grimsby (01472 323345).** Tells the story of fishermen, their boats and the waters they fished in; the dangers and hardships of life at sea are explained.
www.nelincs.gov.uk

NORTHAMPTONSHIRE

◆ **Turner's Musical Merry-go-round, Queen Eleanor Vale, Newport Pagnell Road, Wootton (01604 763314).** Indoor fairground with historic and functioning fairground organs, rides on giant roundabout.

NOTTINGHAMSHIRE

◆ **Sherwood Forest Country Park and Visitor Centre, Near Mansfield (01623 823202).** Includes visitor centre with Robin Hood Exhibition, guided walks, picnic sites, and refreshments.
www.robinhood.co.uk

◆ **Tales of Robin Hood, Nottingham. (0115 9483284).** The latest audio-visual technology transports you through 700 years of history as you ride through Medieval Nottingham.
www.robinhood.uk.com

☆ Fun for all the Family ☆

OXFORDSHIRE

◆ **Blenheim Palace, Woodstock (08700 602080).** Home of the Duke of Marlborough, with magnificent collection of tapestries and porcelain. Landscaped grounds with butterfly house, adventure playground and railway. World Heritage Site.
www.blenheimpalace.com

◆ **Cotswold Wild Life Park, Burford (01993 823006).** A large and varied collection of animals from all over the world in natural surroundings.
www.cotswoldwildlifepark.co.uk

SHROPSHIRE

◆ **Ironbridge Gorge Museum, Telford (01952 432166).** Award-winning museum complex which brings industrial history to life. Working museums and real history - the images and objects of the industrial revolution.
www.ironbridge.org.uk

◆ **Hoo Farm Animal Kingdom, near Telford (01952 677917).** Friendly llamas, inquisitive ostriches, plus lots more. Undercover and outdoor attractions.
www.hoofarm.com

STAFFORDSHIRE

◆ **Alton Towers, Alton (0870 444 4455).** Europe's premier leisure park – rides, gardens, monorail, shops, adventure play areas etc. New interactive adventure ride – Duel.
www.alton-towers.co.uk

◆ **Drayton Manor Theme Park and Zoo, Near Tamworth. (01827 287979).** Over 100 heart stopping range of rides, including Apocalypse, Shockwave and Stormforce 10; nature trail, zoo, parkland and lakes.
www.draytonmanor.co.uk

WARWICKSHIRE

◆ **Heritage Motor Centre, Gaydon (01926 641188).** Purpose-built transport museum containing collection of historic British cars. Site includes four-wheel drive circuit.
www.heritage.org.uk

◆ **The Shakespearian Properties, Stratford-upon-Avon (01789 204016).** Five distinctive homes including Shakespeare's Birthplace and Anne Hathaway's Cottage, all administered by the Shakespeare Birthplace Trust.
www.stratford-upon-avon.co.uk

◆ **Warwick Castle, Warwick (0870 442 2000).** Britain's greatest medieval experience – castle with dungeon, armoury and torture chamber, all set in 60 acres of grounds.
www.warwick-castle.co.uk

WEST MIDLANDS

◆ **National Sea Life Centre, Birmingham (0121-633 4700).** Bringing the magic of the marine world to the heart of Birmingham with over 55 displays of marine and freshwater creatures. Features the world's first 360° fully transparent viewing tunnel.
www.sealife.co.uk

◆ **Thinktank at Millennium Point, Birmingham (0121 202 2222).** 10 themed galleries where you can examine the past, investigate the present, and explore what the future may bring.
www.thinktank.ac

WORCESTERSHIRE

◆ **West Midland Safari & Leisure Park, Spring Grove (01299 402114).** From reptiles to roller coasters – it's all here!
www.wmsp.co.uk

Key to Symbols - see page 4

Please contact individual establishments to ensure that the facilities you require are available.

MIDLANDS
Board

ASHBOURNE • Dog & Partridge Country Inn — *Terms on request*

🛏 30 🛁 28 ⬩ ✕ BB ⬩ 🛏 ⬩ 🐴 ⬩ 🐕 ⬩ 🍷 — Ⓐ

BUXTON • Devonshire Arms — *Terms on request*

✕ BB ⬩ 🐕 🍷 — Ⓐ

BUXTON • Alison Park Hotel — *B&B £45-£50pppn*

🛏 17 🛁 17 ✕ BB ⬩ 🛏 🐕 ♿ 🍷 — Ⓐ ⊘

GREAT MALVERN • Croft Guest House — *Terms on request*

🛏 5 🛁 3 ✕ BB 🐕 🍷 — ⊘

HENLEY-ON-THAMES • The Old Bakery — *Terms on request*

🛏 3 🛁 1 BB 🛏 🐴 🐕 — Ⓐ

MIDLANDS
Self-catering

SKEGNESS • Chestnuts Country Cottages — *Terms on request*

   🐴 🐕 — Ⓐ

STANTON-BY-BRIDGE • Woodland Hills Court Holiday Cottages — *£350-£500 per week*

🏠 📋 🛏 🛁 ♿ — W Ⓐ ⊘

NORTH-EAST ENGLAND

⛰ Best Beaches ⛰

This year no less than 11 beaches on this impressive stretch of coastline have won a European Blue Flag. Several beaches have also gained a Quality Coast Award.

ⓘ North East England Tourism
- Tel: 01904 707961
- Fax: 01904 707070
- www.visitnortheastengland.com

Blue Flag Beaches 2008

- *Tynemouth*
  King Edward's Bay
  Longsands South
- *South Shields, Sandhaven*
- *Whitby West Cliff*
- *Filey*
- *Scarborough North Bay*
- *Bridlington North*
- *Hornsea*
- *Whitley Bay South*
- *Withernsea*
- *Seaton Carew Foreshore*

BRITAIN'S BEST BEACHES
See pages 41-46

For more information about holidaying in the North East see:

www.visitteesvalley.co.uk

www.visitnorthumberland.com

www.visitcountydurham.com

www.visitnewcastlegasteshead.co.uk

BRIDLINGTON

⚏ Family Fun Activities: Summer shows • Children's attractions • Sports and games, golf, boating, fishing, wind-surfing • Indoor Leisure World (4 pools). New: Eye of the Bay (big wheel)

☆ Special Events: May: Week-long festival of street and theatre shows. **August:** Lions Carnival. **September**: Sea angling week. **October:** Carnival Championships.

ℹ Information Centre, 25 Prince Street, Bridlington YO15 2NP • 01262 673474 www.discoveryorkshirecoast.com www.visitbrid.co.uk www.visiteastyorkshire.com

⚓ Beaches

• **NORTH BEACH.** Two miles long, sandy and naturally sheltered, with cliffs and rock pools towards northern end. Promenade; good parking. *Safety and maintenance:* cleaned daily. *Beach facilities:* deck chairs; various entertainments on beach; ice cream kiosks, snack bars, restaurants and pubs; toilets with ♿ access. *Dog restrictions:* banned May to end September, must be kept on lead on Promenade.

• **SOUTH BEACH.** Two miles long, sandy and naturally sheltered with some dunes at southern end. Promenade and good parking. *Safety and maintenance:* cleaned daily. *Beach facilities:* deck chairs; beach chalets for hire; beach activities; donkey rides; ice cream kiosks, snack bars, restaurants and pubs; toilets with ♿ access (open 24 hours in summer). *Dog restrictions:* banned May to end September, must be kept on lead on Promenade.

CLEETHORPES

⚏ Family Fun Activities: Leisure Centre, Pleasure Island Theme Park, Cleethorpes Coast Light Railway, Discovery Centre, The Jungle Zoo; 10-Pin Bowling Centre, Promenade Gardens, Lakeside Sand Pit and Paddling Pool, Fantasy World; Laser Adventure • Crazy golf, amusement arcades, children's entertainment, night clubs, discos.

☆ Special Events: May: Kite Festival. **July/August:** Carnival Week and Parade. Markets: Wednesday and Sunday.

ℹ Tourist Information Centre, Cleethorpes Library, Alexandra Road, Cleethorpes DN35 8LG Tel: 01472 323111 • Fax: 01472 323112 e-mail: cleetic@nelincs.gov.uk www.enjoycleethorpes.com

⚓ Beaches

• **NORTH PROMENADE.** Sandy and naturally sheltered; promenade; good parking. *Safety and maintenance:* Beach Safety Officers; sandbanks; beach cleaned daily. *Beach facilities:* deck chairs; donkeys, swings, Big Wheel, fairground; ice cream kiosks, snack bars, restaurants, pubs; toilets with ♿ ramps. *Dog restrictions:* from 1st April to 30th September dogs are restricted on various clearly marked areas of the beach.

• **CENTRAL PROMENADE.** Three-quarters of a mile long, sandy; naturally sheltered Promenade and good parking. *Safety and maintenance:* cleaned daily; Beach Safety Officers, warning signs. *Beach facilities:* deck chairs; donkeys, horses and carts, land train; ice cream kiosks, snack bars, pubs; toilets with ♿ ramps. *Dog restrictions:* from April 1st to 30th September dogs are restricted on various clearly marked areas of the beach.

FILEY

⛱ Family Fun Activities: Boating lake, putting, crazy golf, trampolines, children's play area, miniature golf • Bird Garden & Animal Park, Folk Museum, Filey Dams Nature Reserve, Filey Brigg Nature Trail, Filey Sculpture Trail.

☆ Special Events: **June/July:** Filey Festival. **July:** Filey Regatta. **August:** Life Boat Day. **August/September:** Fishing Festival.

i Tourist Information Centre, John Street, Filey YO14 9DW
01723 383637 • Fax: 01723 518001
www.discoveryorkshirecoast.com

⛱ Beaches

• **BEACH.** Miles of open sand, naturally sheltered; parking. *Safety and maintenance:* cleaned daily, flagged, warning signs; lifeguards. *Beach facilities:* deckchairs, beach chalets; donkey rides; cafe and ice-cream kiosk; toilets with ♿ access. *Dog restrictions:* banned between Coble Landing and Royal Parade (seasonal).

SCARBOROUGH

⛱ Family Fun Activities: Heated indoor pool, spa, sports centre, crown green bowls, 10-pin bowling, tennis, putting, two golf courses • Mini railway, boating lake, angling in harbour • Amusement arcades, bingo, cinemas, theatre, nightclubs • Museums and 12thC castle • Bird of Prey Centre, Shire Horse Farm, mini "naval warfare", Sea Life Centre, Honey Farm, Terror Tower, pleasure boat trips, Dino Days (Dinosaur Coast events).

i Tourist Information Centre, Sandside, Scarborough YO11 1PP
01723 383637 • Fax: 01723 383604
tourismbureau@scarborough.gov.uk
www.discoveryorkshirecoast.com

☆ Special Events: **May/June:** Scarborough Fayre; festivals, International Music Festival. **July:** Seafest. **September:** Jazz Festival.

⛱ Beaches

• **NORTH BAY BEACH.** Three-quarters of a mile long, sandy with rockpools and cliffs. Promenade, good parking. *Safety and maintenance:* cleaned daily; flagged, warning signs, lifeguards. *Beach facilities:* deck chairs and beach chalets; donkey rides; putting and boating lake. *Dog restrictions:* 1st May to 30th September - no dogs permitted between Scalby Mills and mini roundabout; must be kept on lead on Promenade.

• **SOUTH BAY BEACH.** Half a mile long, sandy and naturally sheltered. Promenade, bay includes Scarborough harbour with three piers. Good parking. *Safety and maintenance:* cleaned daily; flagged, warning signs, lifeguards. *Beach facilities:* deck chairs and beach chalets; donkey rides; swings and roundabouts; toilets with ♿ access. *Dog restrictions:* 1st May to 30th September - no dogs permitted from West Pier to Spa Footbridge.

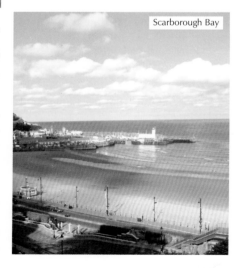

Scarborough Bay

WHITBY

Family Fun Activities: Heated indoor pool, boating, yachting, trout and salmon fishing, putting, crazy golf, golf,; bowls • Leisure Centre • Theatres, pavilion, museum, art gallery • Remains of 11th century abbey, Dracula Experience Trail, Captain Cook Heritage Trail, Funtastic indoor play area.

Special Events: March: Eskdale Festival of Arts. **August:** Whitby Regatta.

i Tourist Information Centre,
Langborne Road, Whitby YO21 1YN
01723 383637 • Fax: 01947 606137
tourismbureau@scarborough.gov.uk
www.discoveryorkshirecoast.com

Beaches

• **BEACH.** Three miles long, sandy and naturally sheltered. Good parking. *Safety and maintenance:* cleaned daily; warning signs, lifeguards. *Beach facilities:* deck chairs and beach chalets; donkey rides; ice cream kiosk and snack bar; toilets with ⅃ access. *Dog restrictions:* May to September – banned between Battery Parade and former Beach Cafe; must be kept on lead on Battery Parade and Promenade.

☆ Fun for all the Family ☆

COUNTY DURHAM

◆ **The Josephine and John Bowes Museum, Barnard Castle (01833 690606).** Outstanding art collection, plus ceramics, porcelain, tapestries, and objects d'art (including Silver Swan automaton).
www.bowesmuseum.org.uk

◆ **Beamish, The North of England Open Air Museum, Beamish (0191 370 4000).** A vivid re-creation of how people lived and worked at the turn of the century. Town Street, Home Farm, Colliery, Railway Station; tram rides, tea rooms.
www.beamish.org.uk

EAST YORKSHIRE

◆ **Elsham Hall Country and Wildlife Park, Near Brigg (01652 688698).** See working craftsmen demonstrate their traditional skills in the craft centre set in beautiful grounds and lakeside gardens. Children's farm, lake, adventure playground, falconry centre.
www.elshamhall.co.uk

◆ **The Deep, Hull (01482 381000).** Discover the story of the world's oceans on a dramatic journey back in time and into the future! The world's only underwater lift and Europe's deepest viewing tunnel!
www.thedeep.co.uk

NORTHUMBERLAND

◆ **Alnwick Castle (01665 510777).** A mighty fortress, seat of the Duke of Northumberland since 1309. Location for the 'Harry Potter' films.
www.alnwickcastle.com

◆ **Grace Darling Museum, Bamburgh (01668 214465).** Many original relics re-create the rescue by Grace and her father of the survivors of the wrecked Forfarshire.

◆ **Leaplish Waterside Park, Kielder Water (01434 220643).** Ideal base for exploring the largest man-made lake in Britain; all sorts of sports, forest playground, restaurant.
www.kielder.org

☆ Fun for all the Family ☆

TEES VALLEY

◆ **Captain Cook Birthplace Museum, Middlesbrough (01642 311211).** Special effects add realism to the museum displays which tell the story of the famous explorer.

◆ **Hartlepool Historic Quay, Hartlepool (01429 860006).** Travel back in time to the sights, sounds and smells of 18th century seaport life. New attractions include children's adventure playship.
www.thisishartlepool.co.uk

◆ **Saltburn Smugglers Heritage Centre, Saltburn-by-the-Sea (01287 625252).** Experience the sights, sounds and smells of Saltburn's dark past in authentic settings.

TYNE & WEAR

◆ **Life Science Centre, Newcastle-upon-Tyne (0191 243 8223).** Discover just how truly amazing life is. Explore where life comes from and how it works. Meet your 4 billion year old family, find out what makes you unique, test your brainpower and enjoy the thrill of the Motion Simulator Ride.
www.lifesciencecentre.org.uk

◆ **Wildfowl and Wetlands Trust, Washington (0191-416 5454).** Have a great day out supporting conservation on a nose-to-beak voyage of discovery – many birds feed from the hand. Exhibition area, tea room, play area.
www.wwt.org.uk

NORTH & WEST YORKSHIRE

◆ **Colour Museum, Bradford (01274 390955).** Examines colour, light and the history of dyeing and textile printing. Interactive galleries and workshops.
www.sdc.org.uk/museum

◆ **Eden Camp Modern History Theme Museum, Malton (01653 697777).** Civilian life in Britain during WWII – experience the sights, sounds and even smells of 1939-1945 at this award-winning museum.
www.edencamp.co.uk

◆ **Flamingo Land Theme Park, Zoo and Holiday Village, off Malton-Pickering Road (0870 7528000).** Rides and slides, zoo, indoor playcentre, cable car ride etc.
www.flamingoland.co.uk

◆ **Lightwater Valley Theme Park, Ripon (0870 458 0040).** The world's longest roller coaster, thrill rides, theatre, crazy golf, boating lake and much more. Restaurant and cafes.
www.lightwatervalley.co.uk

◆ **National Museum of Photography, Film and Television, Bradford (0870 701 0200).** Packed with things to do and find out, this bright, modern museum is a fun day out for all the family, telling the fascinating story of still and moving pictures.
www.nmpft.org.uk

◆ **National Railway Museum, York (01904 621261).** See how Britain's railways shaped the world at the largest railway museum in the world. BR's up to-the-minute exhibit gives a glimpse into the future. Restaurant and gift shop.
www.nrm.org.uk

◆ **Royal Armouries Museum, Leeds (0113-220 1916).** New attraction with thousands of items from a collection previously housed in the Tower of London. Jousting displays, Wild West gun fights, Oriental swordsmanship, plus lots more.
www.armouries.org.uk

Key to Symbols - see page 4
Please contact individual establishments to ensure that the facilities you require are available.

NORTH EAST ENGLAND   Board

DANBY • Rowantree Farm   *Terms on request*

🛏 2 🛁 2   ✕ BB   ▥ 🪑   ⊗

FROSTERLEY-IN-WEARDALE • Newlands Hall   *Terms on request*

🛏 2 🛁 2   BB   ⊗

HALTWHISTLE • Saughy Rigg Farm   *Terms on request*

✕ BB   🐕   Ⓐ

LEYBURN • Sunnyridge   *B&B £28-£33pppn*

🛏 2 🛁 2   BB   ▥   🐕   ⊗

ROTHBURY • Lee Farm   *Terms on request*

🛏 3 🛁 3   BB   🐕   🍷   Ⓐ ⊗

SCARBOROUGH • Terrace Hotel   *Terms on request*

🛏 7 🛁 2   BB   Ⓐ ⊗

NORTH EAST ENGLAND   Self-catering

BERWICK-UPON-TWEED • 2 The Courtyard   *Terms on request*

🏢   🪑 🎠   🐕   ⊗

MORPETH • Micklewood Park   *Terms on request*

🏠   🗒   🎠 ⛺ 🐕 ♿   W Ⓐ

NORTHALLERTON • Otterington Park   *Terms on request*

⛺ 🐕

WHITBY • Middlewood Farm Holiday Park   *Terms on request*

🚐   ⛺ 🐕   ⊗

WHITBY • Greenhouses Farm Cottages   *Terms on request*

🏠   🗒   ⛺

NORTH WEST ENGLAND

Best Beaches

There are lovely stretches of coastline and clean sands, and lively resorts whose efforts to maintain their high place in British holiday planning are showing successful results - St Annes Pier has earned a Quality Coast Award.

i **North West Tourism**
(Cheshire, Greater Manchester, High Peak, Lancashire, Merseyside).

- **e-mail: venw@nwda.cco.uk**
- **www.englandsnorthwest.com**

Blackpool and the Tower

For more information about holidaying in the North West see:

- •www.visitlancashire.com
- •www.visitchester.com
- •www.golakes.co.uk
- •www.visitliverpool.com
- •www.visitmanchester.com

BLACKPOOL

⚤ **Family Fun Activities:** Pleasure Beach with over 145 rides and attractions including Europe's tallest, fastest roller-coaster and Valhalla, the world's biggest dark ride • Blackpool Tower with 7 levels of fun including a circus, ballroom, adventure playground and aquarium • Zoo, Sealife Centre, Sandcastle Waterworld indoor water paradise, Louis Tussaud's Waxworks • Stanley Park with lake, Italian Gardens, bowling, children's playgrounds, putting and Sports Centre • Three piers with arcades, shows and amusements, Winter Gardens with ballroom and Opera House, Grand Theatre • 10-pin bowling, golf, putting, go-karts, fishing, swimming pools • Multiplex cinemas, shows, pubs.

☆ **Special Events: July/August:** Kids MegaFest Children's Festival. **1st September to 5th November:** Blackpool Illuminations.

ℹ️ **Blackpool Tourism, 1 Clifton Street, Blackpool FYI lLY • 01253 478222 e-mail: tourism@blackpool.gov.uk www.visitblackpool.com**

⛰ **Beaches**

• **BEACH.** Approximately 7 miles long, sandy. Promenade, tramcars; good parking. *Safety and maintenance:* foreshore flagged, warning signs; lifeguards; beach cleaned daily. *Beach facilities:* deck chairs, donkey rides; ice cream kiosks, snack bars, restaurants, pubs; toilets with special needs access and mother/baby changing facilities. *Dog restrictions:* banned from the beach between North Pier and South Pier from May to September; must be kept on a lead on every street in Blackpool.

LYTHAM ST ANNES

⚤ **Family Fun Activities:** Heated indoor pool; pier, donkey rides on beach; children's playground, boating lake, floral gardens; tennis, putting, bowls, trampolines; miniature railway; golf courses (4); sailing; pubs, cafes and restaurants; theatre at Lytham; RSPB Discovery Centre at Fairhaven Lake.

☆ **Special Events: May/August:** Carnivals and Fete days, miscellaneous local shows and competitions throughout the year.

ℹ️ **Visitor and Travel Information, Lytham St Annes FY8 ILH 01253 725610 • Fax: 01253 640708**

⛰ **Beaches**

• **BEACH.** Sandy, three miles long, and backed by dunes and promenade. Pier with arcade and refreshments. Good parking. *Safety and maintenance:* patches of soft sand and mud; river estuary; warning signs. Cleaned daily in season. *Beach facilities:* deck chairs, donkey rides; ice cream kiosks, snack bars, restaurants; toilets with ♿ access. *Dog restrictions:* can be exercised north of St. Annes pier, past the high water mark.

MORECAMBE

⚐ Family Fun Activities: Happy
Mount Park (including Splash Park),
Superbowl, Megazone and Cinema
• Promenade and play areas, Stone Jetty
with seabird-themed pavement games,
arcades and amusements.
See our family-fun page:
**www.citycoastcountryside.co.uk/site/what
-to-see-and-do/family-fun**

✫ Special Events: Free family events
include: **July:** Catch the Wind Kite Festival.
August: Sandcastle Festival. **September:**
"We do like to be beside the seaside".

[*i*] **Morecambe Visitor Information
Centre, Old Station Buildings, Marine
Road Central, Morecambe LA4 4DB
01524 582808 • Fax: 01524 832549
e-mail: morecambetic@lancaster.gov.uk
www.citycoastcountryside.co.uk**

⚐ Beaches
• **BEACH.** Several stretches of sand, backed
by 5 mile long flat promenade with
beautiful views across the wide expanse of
Morecambe Bay towards the Lake District.
Ample parking. *Safety and maintenance:*
safety signs and lifebelts; Promenade
Supervisor. *Beach facilities:* ice cream kiosks;
toilets incl. some with ♿ access; miniature
train. *Dog restrictions:* dogs not allowed on
amenity beaches.

✫ Fun for all the Family ✫

CHESHIRE

◆ **Blue Planet Aquarium, Ellesmere Port
(0151 357 8804).** The UK's largest
aquarium with moving walkway through
tropical fish and a large collection of sharks.
www.blueplanetaquarium.com

◆ **Boat Museum, Ellesmere Port (0151-
355 5017).** World's largest floating
collection of canal craft on a 7-acre site.
Steam engines, blacksmith's forge etc. Cafe.
www.boatmuseum.org.uk

◆ **Brookside Miniature Railway, Poynton
(01625 872919).** Cheshire's greatest little
railway. Super train rides, authentic detail in
half-mile circuit of gardens. Restaurant.
www.brookside-miniature.railway.co.uk

◆ **Catalyst, Widnes (0151-420 1121).**
Science and technology comes alive with
hands-on exhibits, observatory. The only
science centre solely devoted to chemistry,
with over 30 interactive exhibits.
www.catalyst.org.uk

◆ **Chester Zoo, Chester (01244 380280).**
Britain's largest zoo outside London. Spacious
enclosures. Restaurants and cafeteria.
www.chesterzoo.org.uk

◆ **Jodrell Bank Science Centre, Planetarium
and Arboretum, Near Macclesfield (01477
571339).** 'Hands on' gallery and space
exhibition; planetarium. Lovell Radio Telescope.
www.jb.man.ac.uk

☆ Fun for all the Family ☆

CUMBRIA

◆ **Cars of the Stars Motor Museum, Keswick (017687 73757).** Celebrity TV and film vehicles including Chitty Chitty Bang Bang and the Batmobile plus film set displays.
www.carsofthestars.com

◆ **The Cumberland Pencil Museum, Southey Works, Keswick (017687 73626).** The first-ever pencils were produced in Keswick and the museum traces the history of this everyday writing instrument. See the longest pencil in the world.
www.pencils.co.uk

◆ **Eden Ostrich World, Penrith (01768 881771).** See these magnificent birds in the setting of a real farm on the banks of the River Eden. Play areas, farm animals.
www.ostrich-world.com

◆ **Lake District National Park Visitor Centre, Brockhole, Windermere (01539 724555).** Exciting Lake District exhibitions, including the 'Living Lakeland' display. Restaurant and tearooms.
www.lake-district.gov.uk

◆ **Rheged, The Upland Kingdom Discovery Centre. Penrith (01768 868000).** Journey through 2000 years of Cumbria's magic in this new attraction set under a grass-covered roof. Discover the village in the hill.
www.rheged.com

◆ **Windermere Steamboat Museum, Windermere (015394 45565).** A unique collection of Victorian steam launches and other historic craft. Steam launch trips subject to weather and availability.
www.steamboat.co.uk

GREATER MANCHESTER

◆ **The Lowry, Salford (0870 787 5780).** A world-class venue for performing and visual arts. Theatres and galleries.
www.thelowry.com

◆ **Museum of Science and Industry, Manchester (0161-832 2244).** Like no other museum you've ever been in. Xperiment! – interactive science centre; Power Hall; Victorian Sewers – and lots more.
www.msim.org.uk

LANCASHIRE

◆ **Blackpool Tower (01253 292029).** 520 ft high, houses a circus, aquarium, dance hall and other shows. The famous Illuminations start early in September.
www.theblackpooltower.co.uk

◆ **Wildfowl Trust, Martin Mere (01704 895181).** Exotic and native breeds plus thousands of migrant visitors observed from spacious hides.
www.wwt.org.uk

MERSEYSIDE

◆ **The Beatles Story, Liverpool (0151-709 1963).** Re-live the sights and sounds of the Swinging Sixties a magical mystery tour!
www.beatlesstory.com

◆ **World of Glass, St Helens (08707 114466).** The fascinating history of glass-making. Enter the magical mirror maze and explore the cone building tunnels.
www.worldofglass.com

Families are welcome at this Regency Country House in the heart of the Lake District, just a quarter of a mile from Lake Windermere and a short walk from the centre of Ambleside.

Personally managed by the Nixon family for over 40 years, it still retains the comfortable, relaxed atmosphere of a private house and is well known for the friendly ambience and excellent cuisine. The hotel has 16 bedrooms (including 6 family rooms) and 3 family suites, 2 of which are in the grounds.

Guests have free use of a nearby leisure club with children's pool, sauna, steam room and jacuzzi.

ROTHAY MANOR
HOTEL & RESTAURANT

Family rooms have TV and video

Children's High Tea

Cots, high chairs

Baby listening

Non-smoking

All major credit cards accepted

Good Food Guide • Short listed for Cumbria Tourism "Taste" Awards 2008

Rothay Bridge, Ambleside LA22 0EH
Tel: (015394) 33605 • Fax: (015394) 33607
e-mail: hotel@rothaymanor.co.uk • www.rothaymanor.co.uk/family

---

GREEN GABLES
37 Broad Street, Windermere LA23 2AB

AA

A family-owned and run licensed guesthouse in Windermere centrally situated one-minute's walk from village centre with shops, banks and pubs and only five minutes from the station or bus stop. Accommodation comprises two doubles, one family triple/twin and one single room, all en suite; one family (four) and two family triple/twin rooms with private facilities; all with central heating, colour TV, hairdryers, kettles, tea & coffee. Comfortable lounge bar on the ground floor. No smoking in bedrooms. We can book tours and trips for guests and can advise on activities and special interests. B&B from £23 to £30 pppn. Special Winter offers available. Open just about all year round. Contact **Carole Vernon and Alex Tchumak**.

Tel: 015394 43886 • e-mail: greengables@FSBdial.co.uk • e-mail: info@greengablesguesthouse.co.uk

---

Looking for holiday accommodation?
search for details of properties where children are welcome
www.holidayguides.com

Key to Symbols - see page 4
Please contact individual establishments to ensure that the facilities you require are available.

NORTH WEST ENGLAND — Board

AMBLESIDE • **Rothay Manor**	B&B £73-£145pppn
🛏 19 🛁 19 ✕ BB ⛺ 🛏 ⛲	♿ ⚲ W ⊘
LYTHAM ST ANNES • **Chadwick Hotel**	B&B £45-£60pppn
🛏 75 🛁 75 ✕ BB ⛺ 🛏 ⛲ 🐴	♿ ⚲ 🎱 W Ⓐ ⊘
ST ANNES ON SEA • **Dalmeny Hotel**	Terms on request
🛏 120 🛁 120 ✕ BB ⛺ 🛏 ⛲ 🐴 🛝	♿ ⚲ 🎱 W
WINDERMERE • **Green Gables**	Terms on request
🛏 7 🛁 7 BB	⚲ Ⓐ

NORTH WEST ENGLAND — Self-catering

AMBLESIDE • **Ramsteads Coppice**	£220-£450 per week
🏠 🗄 🛏 ⛲	
AMBLESIDE • **Greenhowe Caravan Park**	Terms on request
🚐 🗄 🏠 🛏 🐕	
COCKERMOUTH • **Irton House Farm**	Terms on request
🏠 🗄 🐴 ♿ Ⓐ ⊘	
ESKDALE • **Fisherground Farm**	Terms on request
🏠 🏡 🗄 🐴 🛝 🐕 Ⓐ	

SCOTLAND

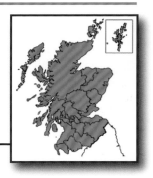

🏔 Best Beaches 🏔

Scotland has a huge coastline, one of the longest in Europe, with great stretches of sand along the Solway, on the Ayrshire coast, East Lothian and Fife, around Aberdeen, along the Moray Firth and in the North West. Good beach management practices have been rewarded with six European Blue Flags. In addition Seaside Awards (Resort and Rural Categories) have gone to beaches which meet the high standards required.

BLUE FLAG BEACHES 2008

- *St Andrews West Sands*
- *Elie Harbour*
- *Aberdour Silver Sands*
- *Leven East*
- *Burntisland*
- *Montrose*

[i] **Scottish Tourist Board**
- **Tel: 0845 2255 121**
- **e-mail: info@visitscotland.com**
- **www.visitscotland.com**

ABERDEEN

Family Fun Activities: Winter Gardens, Art Gallery, museums, cinemas, theatres, Music Hall • Doonies Farm, Hazlehead Park, Aberdeen Fun Beach, Satrosphere Hands-on Science Centre, Storybook Glen • Windsurfing, bowling, squash, tennis, Linx Ice Arena, cricket, rugby, riding, walking, climbing, fishing, golf.

i **Aberdeen Visitor Information Centre, 23 Union Street, Aberdeen AB11 5BP 01224 288828 e-mail: Aberdeen@visitscotland.com www.aberdeen-grampian.com**

Beaches

• **BEACH.** Two and a half miles of sandy beach, promenade and harbour; ample parking. *Safety and maintenance:* cleaned daily; lifeboats, lifebelts; lifeguards in summer. **Aberdeen Fun Beach:** Scotland's largest family entertainment centre, open all year. Restaurants, multi-plex cinema, leisure centre with swimming pool and flumes, ice arena, indoor and outdoor funfair, ten-pin bowling, pool and Ramboland – children's adventure play area

ISLE OF ARRAN

Family Fun Activities: This peaceful island, "Scotland in Miniature", offers a wealth of leisure activities and places of interest including Brodick Castle, Gardens and Country Park, Isle of Arran Distillery, Balmichael Visitor Centre, Isle of Arran Heritage Museum, Arran Aromatics.

i **Tourist Information Centre, The Pier, Brodick KA27 8AU 0845 2255 121 e-mail: Brodick@visitscotland.com www.ayrshire-arran.com**

★ **Special Events:** July: Arran Fleadh. **August:** Highland Games. **October:** Ladies Golf Competition. **November:** Gents Golf Competition.

Beaches

• **BEACHES.** Varied coastline with shingle and pebble shores and sandy beaches suitable for all the family.

AYR

Family Fun Activities: Citadel Leisure Complex • Swimming pool, 10-pin bowling, golf, putting, pitch and putt, cricket, tennis, bowls • Cinema, dancing/discos • Racecourse • Nearby Burns National Heritage Park, Belleisle Park, Rozelle Park, Craig Tara, Heads of Ayr Park.

★ **Special Events: May:** Ayr Agricultural Show. **June:** Ayr Golf Week. **August:** Flower Show. **September:** Ayr Gold Cup (horse racing).

i **Tourist Information Centre, 22 Sandgate, Ayr KA7 1BW 0845 2255 121 e-mail: Ayr@visitscotland.com www.ayrshire-arran.com**

Beaches

• **BEACH.** Two and a half miles long, sand and some shingle; promenade and harbour; ample parking. *Beach facilities:* children's playground, crazy golf, boating pond, putting on promenade; cafes; toilets with & access.

GIRVAN

⚓ **Family Fun Activities:** Swimming pool, golf, putting, tennis, bowls • Boat trips and fishing.

☆ **Special Events:** **May:** Folk Festival. **June:** Civic Week. **August:** Annual Maidens Harbour Gala. **October:** Folk Festival.

🏖 **Beaches**

• **BEACH.** One and a half miles long, sandy and some shingle; promenade and harbour, ample parking. *Beach facilities:* children's playground, boating pond; toilets with & access.

LARGS

⚓ **Family Fun Activities:** Swimming pool, sauna/solarium; tennis, putting, squash, golf, bowling, windsurfing, diving. • Vikingar, Kelburn Castle & Country Centre

☆ **Special Events:** **August:** Regatta Week. **September:** Viking Festival.

ⓘ **Tourist Information Centre, The Station, Largs 0845 2255 121 e-mail: Largs@visitscotland.com www.ayrshire-arran.com**

🏖 **Beaches**

• **BEACH.** Shingle and sand; promenade, parking; boating pond; cafes and ice cream kiosks; toilets with & access.

MILLPORT

⚓ **Family Fun Activities:** Organised children's activities • Tennis, pitch and putt, trampolines, golf, riding, cycle hire, bowling, fun fair • Museum, aquarium at Marine Station • The Cathedral of the Isles (smallest cathedral in Britain). Millport is reached by car/passenger ferry from Largs; 10 minute bus ride from ferry slip to town.

☆ **Special Events:** **July/August:** Country and Western Festival, Cumbrae Weekend.

🏖 **Beaches**

• **BEACH.** Sand and shingle, rock pools; parking. *Beach facilities:* cafes and shops nearby, toilets, some with & access. *Dog restrictions:* must be kept on lead.

TROON

⚓ **Family Fun Activities:** golf, bowling, tennis, swimming, children's play areas.

☆ **Special Events:** **June:** Gala Week.

ⓘ **www.ayrshire-arran.com**

🏖 **Beaches**.

• **BEACH.** Excellent sandy beach with first-aid and life saving equipment nearby. Toilets.

ROTHESAY

Family Fun Activities: Main town on the Isle of Bute easily reached by car/passenger ferry from Wemyss Bay or Colintraive • Pavilion with family variety shows, children's entertainment • Mount Stuart, Isle of Bute Discovery Centre and cinema/theatre, Rothesay Castle, Bute Museum • Putting, tennis, bowling, golf, pony trekking • Leisure Pool with sauna/solarium • Ornamental gardens, castle and museum, walks.

i Isle of Bute Discovery Centre,
**Victoria Street, Rothesay,
Isle of Bute PA20 0AH
0845 2255 121
e-mail: Rothesay@visitscotland.com
www.VisitBute.com**

BRITAIN'S BEST BEACHES
See pages 41-46

ST ANDREWS

Family Fun Activities: Historic University town with 13th century Castle and 12th century Cathedral, St Andrews Museum, St Andrews Aquarium, Craigtoun Country Park, East Sands Leisure Centre • Bowling, tennis, putting, and (of course) GOLF (British Golf Museum) • Theatre, cinema, arts centre. • Fun town tours, sandcastle building competitions (summer months).

i Tourist Information Centre,
**70 Market Street, St Andrews KY16 9NU
01334 472021
e-mail: Standrews@visitscotland.com
www.visitfife.com**

Beaches

• **WEST SANDS.** Wide, flat sandy beach. Within walking distance of town centre, ample parking. *Safety and maintenance:* cleaned regularly and patrolled by council staff; lifeguards during summer months. *Beach facilities:* catering outlets; toilets. *Dog restrictions:* banned from most of beach in summer months; dog exercise area.

• **EAST SANDS.** Sandy beach, just past the harbour; parking. *Safety and maintenance:* cleaned regularly; lifeguards during summer months. *Beach facilities:* catering facilities; watersports; toilets. *Dog restrictions:* banned during summer months.

☆ Fun for all the Family ☆

NORTHERN SCOTLAND

◆ **Anderson's Storybook Glen, Maryculter, near Aberdeen (01224 732941)**. Old Woman's Shoe, Pixie Park, Old MacDonald, play park and the Three Bears' House. Waterfalls.

◆ **Archaeolink Prehistory Park, near Insch (01464 851500)**. All-weather attraction with events inside and out, exhibition and film theatre, all set in 40 acres.
www.archaeolink.co.uk

◆ **Cawdor Castle, Nairn (01667 404401)**. A 14th century Keep, fortified in the 15th century and the 17th century, the massive fortress is set in splendid grounds with nature trails and gardens. Shops, snack bar, picnic area, restaurant and golf course.
www.cawdorcastle.com

◆ **Buckie Drifter Maritime Heritage Centre, Buckie (01542 8346460**. See how the herring industry worked in the past and walk along a re-created 1920's quayside.
www.moray.org/bdrifter

◆ **Eilean Donan Castle, near Kyle of Lochalsh (01599 555202)**. Probably the most photographed castle in Scotland, Eilean Donan stands in a romantic and picturesque setting on Loch Duich.
www.eieandonancastle.com

◆ **Glamis Castle, near Forfar(01307 840393)**. Childhood home of the Queen Mother and birthplace of Princess Margaret. Visitors have a choice of admission to the Castle/grounds/formal garden/coach house /nature trail/picnic areas, including a children's play area.
www.strathmore-estates.co.uk

◆ **Highland Mysteryworld, Glencoe (01855 811660)**. Five fabulous indoor attractions in spectacular setting at foot of Glencoe. Also adventure playground and leisure centre

◆ **Highland Wildlife Park, Kincraig (01540 651270)**. Over 250 acres with red deer, European bison, wild horses, roe deer, Soay sheep, Highland cattle, wandering freely amidst magnificent Highland scenery.
www.highlandwildlifepark.org

◆ **Kylerhea Otter Haven, Kylerhea, Isle of Skye (01320 366322)**. See otters in their natural habitat and view other wildlife from a spacious hide.

◆ **Landmark Visitor Centre, Carrbridge (01479 841613)**. Attractions include tree-top trail, pine forest nature centre, woodland maze and adventure playground with giant slide and aerial walkways.
www.landmark-centre.co.uk

◆ **The Official Loch Ness Monster Exhibition Centre, Drumnadrochit (01456 450573)**. Explore the mysteries surrounding the existence (or not!) of Nessie, the world-famous monster.
www.loch-ness-scotland.com

◆ **Timespan Heritage Centre, Helmsdale (01431 821327)**. Award-winning heritage centre telling the dramatic story of the Highlands. Landscaped garden with collection of rare herbal medicinal plants.
www.timespan.org.uk

☆ Fun for all the Family ☆

CENTRAL SCOTLAND

◆ **Bannockburn Heritage Centre, near Stirling (01786 812664).** Superb audio visual presentation and magnificent equestrian statue of Robert the Bruce.
www.nts.org.uk/bannockburn

◆ **Blair Drummond Safari & Adventure Park (01786 841456).** Drive through animal reserves, monkey jungle. Pets farm – even a boat safari round chimp island – plus rides, amusements .
www.safari-park.co.uk

◆ **British Golf Museum, St Andrews (01334 460046).** Relive all the history and atmosphere of 500 years of golf. Themed galleries feature the tournaments, players and equipment which today's game.
www.britishgolfmuseum.co.uk

◆ **Deep Sea World, North Queensferry (01383 411880).** An underwater safari beneath the Firth of Forth gives a superb view of thousands of fish as they travel along the longest underwater tunnel in the world.
www.deepseaworld.com

◆ **Falkirk Wheel (08700 500208).** A mechanical marvel, the world's only rotating boatlift used to connect the Forth & Clyde and Union canals.
www.thefalkirkwheel.co.uk

◆ **Frigate Unicorn, Victoria Dock, Dundee (01382 200900).** An 1824 wooden, 46 gun frigate; Britain's oldest ship afloat restored as a floating museum.
www.frigateunicorn.org

◆ **Museum of Transport, Kelvin Hall, Glasgow (0141-287 2720).** The oldest cycle in the world, trams, bikes, trains, horse drawn vehicles, special displays, models and more.
www.seeglasgow.com

◆ **New Lanark, Near Lanark (01555 661345).** An insight into the lives of working men and women in this restored conservation village in an attractive situation by the Falls of Clyde. A World Heritage site.
www.newlanark.org

◆ **Our Dynamic Earth, Edinburgh (0131 550 7800).** Charting the Earth's development over the last 4,500 million years with lots of interactive entertainment for adults and children.
www.dynamicearth.co. uk

◆ **St Andrews Sea Life Aquarium (01334 474786).** Hundreds of different species in displays intended to re-create their natural habitat. Includes playful seals and colourful tropical fish.
www.standrewsaquarium.co.uk

◆ **Scottish Fisheries Museum, Anstruther (01333 310628).** A unique record of Scotland's fishing industry. Museum shop and tearoom. Restored fisherman's cottage.
www.scottish-fisheries-museum.org

◆ **Scottish Deer Centre, Over Rankeilour Farm, near Cupar(01337 810391).** Audio visual show. Outdoor and indoor play areas and the chance to study (and stroke) these beautiful animals at close quarters.

☆ Fun for all the Family ☆

SOUTHERN SCOTLAND

◆ **Brodick Castle and Country Park (01770 302202).** Former seat of the Dukes of Hamilton (now NT) with fine examples of silver, porcelain and paintings. Woodland walks, formal garden; ranger service.
www.nts.org.uk/brodick

◆ **Burns National Heritage Park, Alloway (01292 443700).** Burns Cottage Museum, Auld Kirk, Tam O' Shanter Experience, Brig O' Doon, Burns Monument and Gardens — all within half a mile of each other.
www.burnsheritagepark.com

◆ **Culzean Castle and Country Park, By Maybole (01655 884455).** Castle designed by Robert Adam in 1777; park with deer, swans, walled garden, aviary, restaurant and tearoom.
www.nts.org.uk/culzean

◆ **Floors Castle, Kelso (01573 223333).** Scotland's largest inhabited castle with magnificent collections of tapestries, furniture and porcelain. Gift shop and restaurant.
www.floorscastle.com

◆ **Harestanes Countryside Visitor Centre, Jedburgh (01835 830306).** Wildlife garden and temporary exhibitions. Games and puzzles, adventure play area, tearoom, gift shop. Woodland walks.

◆ **Kelburn Castle & Country Centre, Fairlie (01475 568204).** Historic home of the Earls of Glasgow, with beautiful garden walks, tea room, pony trekking, adventure course, children's stockade, pets' corner and The Secret Forest.
www.kelburnecastle.com

◆ **Loudoun Castle Park, Galston (01563 822296).** Fun for all the family, with amusements and rides (including Britain's largest carousel), castle ruin, animals, aviary, restaurant and gift shop.
www.loudouncastle.co.uk

◆ **Magnum Leisure Centre, Irvine (01294 278381).** Swimming pool complex, ice rink, sports hall, bowls hall, fitness suite, fast food outlet, theatre/cinema and soft play area.
www.themagnum.co.uk

◆ **Traquair House, Near Innerleithen (01896 830323).** Oldest inhabited historic mansion in Scotland. Treasures date from 12th century, unique secret staircase to Priest's Room, craft workshop, woodland walks, maze, brewery.

◆ **Thirlestane Castle, Lauder (01578 722430).** Border country life exhibitions in magnificent castle. Historic toys, woodland walk and picnic areas. Tearoom and gift shop.
www.thirlestanecastle.co.uk

◆ **Vikingar! Largs (01475 689777).** Let live Viking guides take you on an enthralling multi-media journey back in time to trace the history of the Vikings in Scotland. Also swimming pool, soft play area, cinema/theatre and cafe/bar.
www.vikingar.co.uk

COLOGIN – a haven in the hills

If you've just got married or just retired, have toddlers in tow or dogs you can't bear to leave at home, or you just want to get away for a break with all the freedom of a self-catering holiday, then we may have just what you are looking for. Our cosy chalets and well appointed lodges offer everything you need for a relaxing country holiday.

One of the most appealing features of Cologin is its peace and tranquillity. With 14 lodges, 4 chalets, Cruachan Cottage and Cologin Farmhouse, we have plenty of different accommodation options. Choose from a cosy one-bedroom chalet or the larger two-bedroomed lodges, including: pet-free, pet-friendly, wheelchair accessible and non-smoking. Or come with friends and book the farmhouse which sleeps up to 15 people.

Our award-winning family-friendly pub and restaurant, *The Barn,* is within easy reach of all our properties. It's a perfect place to unwind and relax. With its unique atmosphere and friendly staff it is the reason why many of Cologin's guests return year after year.

If you love the great outdoors come rain or shine and want to escape from the routine of city life, Cologin is for you. With 17,000 acres of waymarked forest trails above the farm you can enjoy nature at its finest, with glorious scenery and breathtaking views from the summit over Oban Bay to the islands beyond.

Contact us for colour brochure:
Jim and Linda Battison – resident owners
Cologin, Lerags Glen, Oban, Argyll PA34 4SE
Telephone: 01631 564501 • Fax: 01631 566925
e-mail: info@cologin.co.uk
www.cologin.co.uk

COLOGIN
a haven in the hills
STB ★★★–★★★★
Self Catering

Hope Cottage
Durisdeer, Thornhill

Hope Cottage is a picturesque stone cottage situated beside the village green in the peaceful conservation village of Durisdeer near Thornhill, Dumfriesshire.

The perfect place to relax and unwind. Hope Cottage has been comfortably furnished and equipped for 5/6 people with a large secluded garden. Sleeps 6. Towels, linen, heating and electricity included. Pets welcome.

Plenty to see, plenty to explore and plenty to do in any weather for all the family. Fabulous countryside for cycling and if you are a keen mountain biker, nearby Drumlanrig Castle and Ae Forest have biking trails to suit all abilities. The nearby Solway coast with delightful towns like Kirkcudbright provides an alternative day out. If you fancy a day shopping or to get back to city life for a day, an hour in the car or even the train can get you to Edinburgh, Glasgow, Carlisle or Ayr.

Hope Cottage is the perfect place for your holiday, offering peace and tranquillity if it is a restful holiday that you require, or just somewhere to relax after a busy day touring or hill-walking.

For brochure telephone: Mrs S Stannett
01848 331510 • Fax: 01848 331810
e-mail: a.stann@btinternet.com
www.hopecottage.co.uk

Scottish TOURIST BOARD ★★★★ SELF CATERING

Barfad Farmlands

Two stone cottages set in 80 acres of woodland with beaches and beautiful scenery.

THE CHICKEN COOP • sleeps 2 plus cot. Compact open plan kitchen/dining area, double bedroom, shower/ wc.

THE DAIRY • sleeps 4 plus cot and one extra. Large open plan living/dining room with kitchen area, one family room (one double and one single), one single bedroom, sofa bed for one extra. Shower/wc.

Mrs Barker, Barfad Farm, Tarbert, Loch Fyne, Argyll PA29 6YH Tel: 01880 820549

Both cottages include colour TV, laundry room (shared), parking, electric heating, linen and towels; electricity extra.

BOARD

CARRBRIDGE • The Pines Country Guesthouse   B&B £25-£27.50pppn

🛏 4 🛁 4

FORT WILLIAM • Loch Leven Hotel   Terms on request

🛏 12 🛁 12

STANLEY • Newmill Farm   Terms on request

🛏 3 🛁 3

SELF-CATERING

ABERFELDY • Drumcroy Lodges   £225-£450 per week

ARDRISHAIG • Stronachullin Lodge   Terms on request

AVIEMORE • Cairngorm Highland Bungalows   £195-£850 per week

DALBEATTIE • Barend Holiday Village   £330-£825 per week

KIRKWALL • Pickaquoy/Birsay/Point of Ness Sites   Terms on request

OBAN • Cologin   £220-£1350 per week

THORNHILL • Hope Cottage   £350-£475 per week

TARBERT • Barfad Farmlands   £110-£180 per week

WALES

Best Beaches

An outstanding number resort beaches in Wales have been awarded the European Blue Flag for 2008, and an impressive number have received Seaside Awards (Resort and Rural Categories). Seaside Awards are given to well-managed beaches which comply with the legal minimum microbiological standards of water quality.

BLUE FLAG BEACHES 2008

- *Anglesey*
  Benllech, Church Bay, Llanddwyn, Porth Dafarch, Trearddur Bay
- *Gwynedd*
  Abersoch, Pwllheli, Fairbourne, Dinas Dinlle, Tywyn
- *North Wales*
  Llandudno (North Shore), Llandudno (West Shore), Penmaenmawr, Prestatyn, Rhos-on-Sea/Colwyn Bay
- *Carmarthenshire*
  Pembrey Country Park, Pendine
- *Ceredigion*
  Aberystwyth (North), Aberystwyth (South), New Quay (Harbour), Borth
- *Pembrokeshire*
  Broadhaven (North), Dale, Saundersfoot, Lydstep, Tenby (Castle), Tenby (South), Tenby (North), St Davids (Whitesands), Poppit Sands, Newgale, Newport
- *South Wales*
  Porthcawl (Rest Bay), Port Eynon, Trecco Bay, Barry (Whitmore Bay)

i VisitWales
- **Tel: 08708 300306**
- **Fax: 08701 211259**
- **e-mail: info@visitwales.com**
- **www.visitwales.co.uk**

ABERYSTWYTH

⛩ **Family Fun Activities:** Sports and leisure centre, swimming pools, children's playgrounds, parks, promenade, outdoor paddling pool • Narrow gauge railway, electric cliff railway, camera obscura, marina, castle, hill fort, National Library of Wales, museum, theatre, cinema • Nature reserves and forestry centres, farm park, boat trips, coastal paths, cycle path.

i **Tourist Information Centre, Terrace Road, Aberystwyth SY23 2AG
01970 612125 • Fax: 01970 626566
aberystwythtic@ceredigion.gov.uk
www.tourism.ceredigion.gov.uk**

🏖 Beaches

• **BEACH.** Two-award-winning sloping beaches of coarse grey sand and shingle; North Beach fronted by promenade, parking on sea front; South Beach has ample parking. *Safety and maintenance:* water quality on both beaches usually good. Beach Officer/lifeguard usually on duty July/August. *Beach facilities:* rock pools, donkey rides; paddling pool etc on promenade; restaurants and kiosks; toilets. *Dog restrictions:* dogs banned between 1st May and 30th September on North Beach between jetty and Constitution Hill, and on South Beach between Castle headland and first groyne on South Marine Terrace

COLWYN BAY & RHOS-ON-SEA

⛩ **Family Fun Activities:** Welsh Mountain Zoo, Eirias Park with leisure centre, swimming pool, picnic and play areas, boating lake, model yacht pond, indoor tennis centre and skateboarding area • Pier and promenade with cycle track, Puppet Theatre, cricket ground and children's outdoor paddling pool at Rhos-on-Sea • Angling, bowling, golf, walking, watersports • Theatre/cinema with shows all year round.

☆ **Special Events: May Bank Holiday:** Bay of Colwyn Promenade Day. **August:** Festive Fridays - every Friday in August.

i **Colwyn Bay Touch Screen, Imperial Buildings, Prince's Drive, Colwyn Bay. Tourist Information Point, Happy Faces Centre, Promenade, Rhos-on-Sea
www.visitcolwynbay.org.uk**

🏖 Beaches

• **BEACH.** Sandy beach with easy access along A55 expressway. *Beach facilities:* kiosks; ♿ toilets operate using RADAR Key.

BRITAIN'S BEST BEACHES
See pages 41-46

FHG Guides
**publish a large range of well-known accommodation guides.
We will be happy to send you details or you can use
the order form at the back of this book.**

LLANDUDNO

⚓ **Family Fun Activities:** Pier • putting, paddling pool, indoor swimming pool, yacht pond • Alice in Wonderland memorial on West Shore promenade, tramway and cable car to Great Orme Country Park and Visitor Centre, Great Orme Copper Mines, boat trips, Punch & Judy, 10-pin bowling • Llandudno Museum, Alice in Wonderland Visitor Centre, Bodafon Farm Park, Ski & Snowboard Centre with toboggan run • Theatre, art gallery • Victorian shopping centre.

☆ **Special Events: May Bank Holiday:** Victorian Extravaganza. **June:** Gwyl Llandudno Festival - a summer arts festival. **July:** vehicle rally; Fun day, Bodafon Fields; various promenade events. **November:** Celtic Winter Fayre.

[i] **Tourist Information Centre, Chapel Street, Llandudno LL30 2UY 01492 876413 e-mail: llandudnotic@conwy.gov.uk www.llandudno-tourism.co.uk**

🏖 **Beaches**

• **NORTH SHORE BEACH.** Two miles long, sand and shingle, naturally sheltered; promenade and pier with amusements etc. *Safety and maintenance:* safe bathing beach. *Beach facilities:* deck chairs, donkey rides; pub and hotels on promenade; ice cream kiosks, snack bars etc nearby; toilets with ♿ access at eastern end.

• **WEST SHORE BEACH.** Sandy beach, one mile long; promenade and parking. *Safety and maintenance:* warning signs (sand banks can be dangerous on incoming tide). *Beach facilities:* children's play area; snack bar.

PORTHCAWL

⚓ **Family Fun Activities:** A variety of activities ranging from sports to all the fun of the fair.

☆ **Special Events: February:** Celtic Festival of Wales. **April:** Porthcawl Jazz Festival. **July/August:** Porthcawl Town Carnival; Sea Festival. **September:** Elvis Festival.

[i] **Heritage Coast Tourist Information Centre, Old Police Station, John Street, Porthcawl CF36 3DT • 01656 786639 e-mail: porthcawltic@bridgend.gov.uk www.visitbridgend.com**

🏖 **Beaches**

• **BEACHES.** Trecco Bay and Rest Bay offer miles of golden sands; parking and good disabled access. *Beach facilities:* deckchairs; cafes and ice-cream kiosks; toilets nearby in town. *Dog restrictions:* banned in summer from June onwards.

TENBY

⚓ **Family Fun Activities:** Safe, sandy beaches • Leisure centre, amusement arcade, bowls, putting, sailing, pony trekking, golf courses• Pavilion (plays, variety shows, dancing, concerts etc), male voice choir concerts • Museum and art gallery, 15th century Tudor Merchant's House, aquarium, art galleries • The town is pedestrianised during July and August.

☆ **Special Events:** Air Sea Rescue and Helicopter Displays; Winter and Summer Carnivals, brass bands, Arts Festival.

[i] **Information Centre, Tenby 01834 842402 tenby.tic@pembrokeshire.gov.uk**

☆ Fun for all the Family ☆

NORTH WALES

◆ **Alice in Wonderland Centre, Llandudno (01492 860082).** Pop down the rabbit hole and see the Alice story come to life in colourful scenes. Souvenir shop. A must for all Lewis Carroll fans.
www.wonderland.co.uk

◆ **Anglesey Sea Zoo, Brynsiencyn (01248 430411).** Meet the fascinating creatures that inhabit the seas and shores around Anglesey; adventure playground, children's activities, shops and restaurants.
www.angleseyseazoo.co.uk

◆ **Bodafon Farm Park, Llandudno (01492 549060).** Enjoy a tractor/trailer ride around the paddocks and see the variety of rare breed animals, including shire horses, llamas, and peacocks. Shop, cafe and adventure playground.
www.bodafon.co.uk

◆ **Electric Mountain Visitor Centre, Llanberis (01286 870636).** Discover the amazing powers of hydro-electricity in an exciting and interactive environment.
www.electricmountain.co.uk

◆ **Henblas Park, Bodorgan (01407 840440).** Situated in the heart of Anglesey, with lots to see and do - shearing demonstrations, duck display, indoor adventure playground, farm animals - entertainment for the whole family, whatever the weather.
www.parc-henblas-park.co.uk

◆ **Knights Cavern, Rhyl (01745 338562).** Spine chilling walk through supernatural, mythological Wales. "Tortures in the Castle" is guaranteed to shiver your timbers!

◆ **Museum of Childhood Memories, Beaumaris (01248 712498).** Over 2000 items in themed rooms will delight and fascinate all ages – from teddy bears to clockwork trains.

◆ **Pili Palas, Anglesey (01248 712474).** Exotic butterflies and birds in natural settings, plus (the children's favourites!) creepy crawlies and reptiles. Picnic area, cafe and adventure playground.
www.pilipalas.co.uk

◆ **Sea Life Centre, Rhyl (01745 344660).** Spectacular underwater tunnel allows you to walk through sharks, stingrays and other sea creatures. Regular talks, feeding displays and demonstrations; gift shop.
www.rhyl.com/sealife

◆ **Snowdon Mountain Railway, Llanberis (0870 458 0033).** Travel by train on Britain's only rack and pinion railway up Snowdon. the highest mountain in England and Wales. A masterpiece of Victorian engineeering.
www.snowdonrailway.co.uk

◆ **Sygun Copper Mine, Beddgelert (01766 890595).** Stalagmites and stalactites formed from ferrous oxide. Award-winning attraction with underground audio visual tours.
www.syguncoppermine.co.uk

◆ **Welsh Mountain Zoo, Colwyn Bay (01492 532938).** Magnificent animals in natural surroundings, plus Chimpanzee World, Jungle Adventureland and Tarzan Trail, children's farm, etc - a great day out.
www.welshmountainzoo.org

☆ Fun for all the Family ☆

MID WALES

◆ **Borth Animalarium, Borth (01970 871224).** Domestic and farm animals in the petting barn; exoic and endangered species in large enclosures. Pony rides and handling sessions. Indoor and outdoor play areas; cafe and shop
www.animalarium.co.uk

◆ **Centre for Alternative Technology, Machynlleth (01654 705950).** A "green" village with displays of sustainable and renewable sources of power eg solar, wind. Energy saving houses, organic gardens, bookshop. Adventure playground, restaurant.
www.cat.org.uk

◆ **Chwarel Hen Slate Caverns, Llanfair, Near Harlech (01766 780247).** Self-guided tours of awesome series of slate caverns – spooky in places, but memorable. Also children's farmyard.

◆ **Felinwynt Rainforest and Butterfly Centre, Rhosmaen, Near Aberporth (01239 810882).** Exotic butterflies flying freely in a hothouse atmosphere amid tropical plants and the taped sounds of a Peruvian rainforest.
www.felinwyntrainforest.co.uk

◆ **King Arthur's Labyrinth, Machynlleth (01654 761584).** Sail along an underground river into a world of mystery, legends and storytelling. Also Bards' Quest maze and Corris Craft Centre with many original crafts and workshops. Cafe, outdoor play area.
www.kingarthurslabyrinth.co.uk

◆ **Llywernog Silver-Lead Mine, Ponterwyd, Aberystwyth (01970 890620).** Underground tours and miners' trail telling the story of the hunt for gold and silver in the Welsh hills.
www.silverminetours.co.uk

◆ **Portmeirion Italianate Village, Near Penrhyndeudraeth (01766 770000).** The most "un-Welsh" village in Wales, with the atmosphere of a strange, self-contained world. Location of 'The Prisoner' TV series in the mid-60s.
www.portmeirion.wales.com

◆ **Talyllyn Railway, Tywyn (01654 710472).** Historic steam-operated railway which runs through 7 miles of beautiful countryside, past the scenic Dolgoch Falls, to Abergynolwyn and Nant Gwernol. Railway shop, museum and tearoom.
www.talyllyn.co.uk

☆ Fun for all the Family ☆

SOUTH WALES

◆ **Big Pit, Blaenavon (01495 790311).** Don a miner's helmet and go down a real coal mine with ex-miners as guides. See the stables where the pit ponies were kept. www.nmgw.ac.uk/bigpit

◆ **Cardiff Castle (029 2087 8100).** Spanning nearly 2000 years of history, the splendidly decorated apartments are set in a magnificent building surrounded by eight-acre grounds. www.cardiff.gov.uk

◆ **The Dinosaur Experience, Great Wedlock (01834 845272).** Unique Visitor Centre in 33 acre park, with life-size models, dinosaur trail, hands-on activities; restaurant; picnic areas.

◆ **Grove Land, Near Carmarthen (01994 231181).** Indoor and outdoor activities for all the family — laser clay pigeon shoot, bumper boats, fun barn, play area, pony rides and lots more.

◆ **Heron's Brook Animal Park, Narberth (01834 860723).** Set in 30 acres of parkland, where friendly animals roam freely. Feed the rabbits and guinea pigs at Bunny World, enjoy a round of croquet or putting. www.herons-brook.co.uk

◆ **Manor House Wild Animal Park, St Florence, Tenby (01646 651201).** Pretty grounds with apes, monkeys, otters, deer and an aquarium plus giant slide, radio-controlled boats and other amusements. www.manorhousewildanimalpark.co.uk

◆ **Oakwood, Narberth (01834 891373).** There's a whole voyage of discovery just waiting to set sail at Oakwood. With more than 40 rides and attractions set in 80 acres of landscaped gardens and parkland, there are absolutely no constraints on fun! www.oakwood-leisure.com

◆ **Rhondda Heritage Park, Trehafod (01443 682036).** See the story of Black Gold unfold as you tour the site, set in former working colliery. Underground tour, display, visitor centre, tearoom and gift shop. www.rhonddaheritagepark.com

◆ **Techniquest, Cardiff (029 2047 5475).** Where science and technology come to life - visitors are actively encouraged to handle the exhibits. www.tquest.org.uk

◆ **Tredegar House, Newport (01633 815880).** "Upstairs, Downstairs" tour, adventure playground, craft workshops, boating lake – something for all the family.

Caldicot Castle & Country Park, Near Chepstow (01291 420241). Explore the castle's fascinating past with an audio tour, and take in the breathtaking views of the 55-acre grounds from the battlements. Children's activity centre, play area. www.caldicotcastle.co.uk

Cantref Adventure Farm, Brecon (01874 665223). Award-winning family attraction with live shows, tractor and trailer rides,new paddle boats and electronic tractors, indoor play area, and Europe's longest sledge ride. www.cantref.com

FREE AND REDUCED RATE HOLIDAY VISITS!
Don't miss our Readers' Offer Vouchers on pages 9-40

Cosy cottage in lovely Border countryside,
two miles from Offa's Dyke
• Central heating, washing machine,
dishwasher, microwave, colour TV, inglenook,
woodburner, linen included
• Power shower over bath • Sleeps 4 plus cot
• Ample parking • Sun-trap garden with
Wendy house • On working farm in peaceful
hamlet • Children and pets welcome.

**MRS R. L. JONES, UPPER HOUSE,
KINNERTON, NEAR PRESTEIGNE
POWYS LD8 2PE • Tel: 01547 560207**

BOARD

ABERDOVEY • Trefeddian Hotel *Terms on request*

🛏 59 🐷 59 ♨ ✕ BB 🍴 🛏 ♿ 🐴 ⚖ 🍷 🏊

SELF-CATERING

CAERNARFON • Dinlle Caravan Park *Terms on request*

🚐 🐴 ⚖ 🐕 🍷 🏊

HAVERFORDWEST • Scamford Caravan Park *£150–£475 per week*

🚐 🏠 🛏 ♿ ⚖ 🐕

HAVERFORDWEST • Haven Cottages *Terms on request*

🚐 🏠 📑 🛏 ♿ 🐕

LLANTEG • Llanteglos Estate *Terms on request*

🏠 🛏 ⚖ 🐕 🍷

TREARRDUR BAY • Trearddur Holiday Bungalows *Terms on request*

🏠 📑 🧺 ⚖ 🐕 🍷 🏊

PRESTEIGNE • Whitehall Cottage *£150–£360 per week*

🏠 📑 🛏 ♿ 🐕 Ⓐ

Family-Friendly Pubs & Inns

This is a selection of establishments which make an extra effort to cater for parents and children. The majority provide a separate children's menu or they may be willing to serve small portions of main course dishes on request; there are often separate outdoor or indoor play areas where the junior members of the family can let off steam while Mum and Dad unwind over a drink.

NB: Not all of the establishments featured here have a listing in the main section of this book.

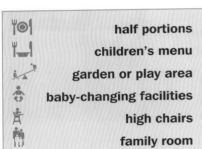

half portions

children's menu

garden or play area

baby-changing facilities

high chairs

family room

THE WELLINGTON ARMS

203 Yorktown Road, Sandhurst,
Berkshire GU47 9BN
Tel: 01252 872408
www.thewellingtonarms.co.uk

VICTORIA INN

Perranuthnoe, Near Penzance,
Cornwall TR20 9NP
Tel: 01736 710309
www.victoriainn-penzance.co.uk

CROOKED INN

Stoketon Cross, Trematon,
Saltash, Cornwall PL12 4RZ
Tel: 01752 848177
www.crooked-inn.co.uk

KINGS ARMS HOTEL

Hawkshead, Ambleside,
Cumbria LA22 0NZ
Tel: 015394 36372
www.kingsarmshawkshead.co.uk

EAGLE & CHILD INN

Kendal Road, Staveley,
Cumbria LA8 9LP
Tel: 01539 821320
www.eaglechildinn.co.uk

MARDALE INN

St Patrick's Well, Bampton,
Cumbria CA19 2RQ
Tel: 01931 713244
www.mardaleinn.co.uk

GILPIN BRIDGE

Bridge End, Levens,
Near Kendal, Cumbria LA8 8EP
Tel: 015395 52206
www.gilpinbridgeinn.co.uk

GREYHOUND HOTEL

Main Street, Shap, Penrith,
Cumbria CA10 3PW
Tel: 01931 716474
www.greyhoundshap.co.uk

QUEEN'S HEAD

Main Street, Hawkshead,
Cumbria LA22 0NS
Tel: 015394 36271
www.queensheadhotel.co.uk

DOLPHIN INN

Kingston, Near Kingsbridge,
Devon TQ7 4QE
Tel: 01548 810314
www.dolphin-inn.co.uk

MALTSTERS ARMS

Bow Creek, Tuckenhay,
Near Totnes, Devon TQ9 7EQ
Tel: 01803 732350
www.tuckenhay.com

THE CRICKETERS

Clavering, Near Saffron Walden,
Essex CB11 4QT
Tel: 01799 550442
www.thecricketers.co.uk

KING'S HEAD INN

Birdwood, Near Huntley,
Gloucestershire GL19 3EF
Tel: 01452 750348
www.kingsheadbirdwood.co.uk

RHYDSPENCE INN
Whitney-on-Wye, Near Hay-on-Wye,
Herefordshire HR3 6EU
Tel: 01497 831262
www.rhydspence-inn.co.uk

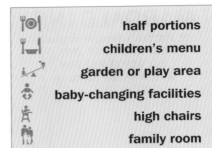
half portions
children's menu
garden or play area
baby-changing facilities
high chairs
family room

SARACENS HEAD INN
Symonds Yat East, Ross-on-Wye,
Herefordshire HR9 6JL
Tel: 01600 890435
www.saracensheadinn.co.uk

CHEQUERS INN
The Street, Smarden,
Near Ashford, Kent TN27 8QA
Tel: 01233 770217
www.thechequerssmarden.com

WHITE HORSE INN
The Street, Boughton,
Kent ME13 9AX
Tel: 01227 751343
www.whitehorsecanterbury.co.uk

WHIPPER-IN HOTEL
Market Place, Oakham,
Leicestershire & Rutland LE15 6DT
Tel: 01572 756971
www.brook-hotels.co.uk

COOK AND BARKER
Newtown-on-the-Moor, Morpeth,
Northumberland NE65 9JY
Tel: 01665 575234
www.cookandbarkerinn.co.uk

TOLLGATE INN
Church Street, Kingham,
Oxfordshire OX7 6YA
Tel: 01608 658389
www.thetollgate.com

THE FLOWER POT
Ferry Lane, Henley-on-Thames,
Oxfordshire RG9 3DG
Tel: 01491 574721

MYTTON AND MERMAID
Atcham, Shrewsbury,
Shropshire SY5 6QG
Tel: 01743 761220
www.myttonandmermaid.co.uk

THE LAMB INN
High Street, Hindon
Wiltshire SP3 6DP
Tel: 01747 820573
www.lambathindon.co.uk

FAIRFAX ARMS
Gilling East, York,
North Yorkshire YO62 4JH
Tel: 01439 788212
www.fairfaxarms.co.uk

CARISBROOKE
Drumduan Road, Forres,
Aberdeen, Banff & Moray IV36 1BS
Tel: 01309 672585
www.carisbrooke-hotel.co.uk

ABERDOUR HOTEL
38 High Street, Aberdour,
Fife KY3 0SW
Tel: 01383 860325
www.aberdourhotel.co.uk

YANN'S AT GLENEARN HOUSE
Perth Road, Crieff,
Perth & Kinross PH7 3EQ
Tel: 01764 650111
www.yannsatglenearnhouse.com

CASTLE VIEW HOTEL
16 Bridge Street, Chepstow,
Monmouthshire NP16 5EZ
Tel: 01291 620349
www.hotelchepstow.co.uk

Index of towns and sections

Please also refer to Contents page 3

FHG Guides Ltd have a large range of attractive holiday accommodation guides for all kinds of holiday opportunities throughout Britain. They also make useful gifts at any time of year. Our guides are available in most bookshops and larger newsagents but we will be happy to post you a copy direct if you have any difficulty. POST FREE for addresses in the UK. We will also post abroad but have to charge separately for post or freight.

£7.99

500 Great Places to Stay
in Britain
• Coast & Country Holidays
• Full range of family accommodation

£8.99

Bed & Breakfast Stops
in Britain
• For holidaymakers and business travellers
• Overnight stops and Short Breaks

£9.99

The Golf Guide
Where to play, Where to stay.
• Over 2800 golf courses in Britain with convenient accommodation.
• Holiday Golf in France, Portugal, Spain, USA and Thailand.

£9.99

The Original Pets Welcome!
• The bestselling guide to holidays for pets and their owners

£6.99

Country Hotels
of Britain
• Hotels with Conference, Leisure and Wedding Facilities

£7.99

Caravan & Camping Holidays
in Britain
• Campsites and Caravan parks
• Facilities fully listed

£6.99

£8.99

£7.99

Pubs & Inns
of Britain
• Including Dog-friendly Pubs
• Accommodation, food and
traditional good cheer

□

Self-Catering Holidays
in Britain
• Cottages, farms, apartments
and chalets
• Over 400 places to stay

□

Weekend & Short Breaks
in Britain
• Accommodation for holidays
and weekends away

□

Tick your choice above and send your order and payment to

FHG Guides Ltd. Abbey Mill Business Centre
Seedhill, Paisley, Scotland PA1 1TJ
TEL: 0141- 887 0428 • FAX: 0141- 889 7204
e-mail: admin@fhguides.co.uk

FHG
·K·U·P·E·R·A·R·D·

Deduct 10% for 2/3 titles or copies; 20% for 4 or more.

Send to: NAME ....

            ADDRESS ....

            ....

            ....

            POST CODE ....

I enclose Cheque/Postal Order for £ ....

            SIGNATURE ....DATE ....

Please complete the following to help us improve the service we provide.

How did you find out about our guides?:

□Press   □Magazines   □TV/Radio   □Family/Friend   □Other